MW01292246

The Battle of South Mountain: The History of the Civil War Battle that Led the Union and Confederate Armies to Antietam

By Charles River Editors

Illustration depicting the fighting at Fox's Gap during the Battle of South Mountain

About Charles River Editors

Charles River Editors is a boutique digital publishing company, specializing in bringing history back to life with educational and engaging books on a wide range of topics. Keep up to date with our new and free offerings with this 5 second sign up on our weekly mailing list.

We make these books for you and always want to know our readers' opinions, so we encourage you to leave reviews and look forward to publishing new and exciting titles each week!

Introduction

A depiction of Confederate casualties at South Mountain

The Battle of South Mountain

"Those in whose judgment I rely tell me that I fought the battle splendidly and that it was a masterpiece of art. ... I feel I have done all that can be asked in twice saving the country. ... I feel some little pride in having, with a beaten & demoralized army, defeated Lee so utterly." - George McClellan

The bloodiest day in American history took place on the 75th anniversary of the signing of the Constitution. On September 17, 1862, Robert E. Lee's Confederate Army of Northern Virginia fought George McClellan's Union Army of the Potomac outside Sharpsburg along Antietam Creek. That day, nearly 25,000 would become casualties, and Lee's army would barely survive fighting the much bigger Northern army. Although the battle was tactically a draw, it resulted in forcing Lee's army out of Maryland and back into Virginia, making it a strategic victory for the North and an opportune time for President Abraham Lincoln to issue the Emancipation Proclamation, freeing all slaves in the rebellious states.

When discussing the Civil War in Maryland, most of the focus is understandably on Antietam, but it's important not to overlook the battle that ultimately brought the Union and Confederate to Antietam Creek in the first place. The Battle of South Mountain was an opening salvo of sorts before Antietam, fought on September 14, 1862 among several gaps. An extension of the Blue Ridge Range, South Mountain was a heavily wooded and rocky terrain that ran southwest from Pennsylvania down to the Potomac River near Harpers Ferry. To the east of the mountain was the town of Frederick, Maryland, less than 50 miles from Washington, D.C.

Lee had defeated McClellan months earlier on the Virginian Peninsula, and he had defeated

John Pope's army weeks earlier at Manassas, but he made a nearly fatal error by dividing his army into several parts across Maryland. While he thought he could do so with McClellan cautiously pursuing him, he could not have known that a copy of the Confederate marching orders would be discovered by Union soldiers at Frederick, Maryland, giving the enemy the Confederates' dispositions. As a result, McClellan's army began moving at an uncharacteristically fast pace in chase of Lee as the already outnumbered Confederates were scattered too far away to assist each other in a general battle.

That first major battle would come at South Mountain, when Union forces tried to push through several gaps on September 14. While Stonewall Jackson's men were busy handling the surrender of Harpers Ferry, Lee only had a few divisions to keep the Northerners from pushing through and in on the rest of his army, which was in critical danger of being surrounded and overwhelmed.

Despite being significantly outnumbered, Lee's army had the advantage of fighting defensively on higher terrain. At Crampton's Gap, Union General William Franklin's nearly 13,000 strong VI Corps crashed down on about 2,000 Confederates led by Howell Cobb who were part of Lafayette McLaws' division. McClellan had ordered Franklin's corps to set out for Crampton's Gap on the morning of September 14, wasting nearly 11 hours in the process, and Franklin delayed his assault for 3 more hours while arranging his lines for what turned out to be a short fight.

The fighting that occurred on that long Sunday was fierce and constant. Artillery, musket, bayonet, and fists were all employed as weapons, resulting in a tremendous number of casualties. The Union forces engaged that day totaled 28,000 and by nightfall 2,325 were listed as casualties. The Confederate Army utilized 18,000 troops and suffered a loss of 2,685 men, an astounding 800 of which were listed as missing. By barely holding onto some of the passes, Lee was able to retreat to Sharpsburg, where he hoped to gather together his scattered forces. As it turned out, the last of the Confederates, A.P. Hill's Light Division, would only arrive around Sharpsburg during the afternoon on September 17, while the Battle of Antietam was at its peak and Lee's army was in danger of being surrounded and captured in its entirety.

Thus, these men, many of whom are lost to history, engaged in a battle that led directly to the bloodiest single day in U.S. military history a few days later along Antietam Creek, and that battle would eventually compel President Lincoln to issue the Emancipation Proclamation. The Battle of South Mountain, therefore, proved to be the catalyst for events that forever altered the course of the Civil War and the nation.

The Battle of South Mountain: The History of the Civil War Battle that Led the Union and Confederate Armies to Antietam looks at the events that led up and brought on the Battle of South Mountain. Along with pictures of important people and places, you will learn about South Mountain like never before.

Chapter Overview

Chapter 1: The Decision to Invade Maryland

This chapter traces the previous months of the war and what compelled Confederate general Robert E. Lee to lead his gray army into a Northern state for the first time.

Chapter 2: Initial Movements

Chapter 2 looks at the two armies' early movements across Maryland in early September, and explains how the Lost Order changed the course of the campaign.

Chapter 3: Harpers Ferry

Chapter 3 covers the siege of Harpers Ferry conducted by Stonewall Jackson, and how this action meant his men wouldn't be on hand to defend South Mountain

Chapter 4: Fox's Gap

Chapter 4 covers the fighting at Fox's Gap, where the heavily outnumbered Confederates put up a desperate resistance to keep their line from a complete collapse

Chapter 5: Turner's Gap

Turner's Gap was also bitterly contested, and this chapter explains the fighting that took place during much of the night. It also chronicles the actions of the Iron Brigade and explains how the legendary Union brigade got its eternal nickname.

Chapter 6: Crampton's Gap

Crampton's Gap was the most crucial part of the battle, and also the most controversial and climactic. This chapter details the sharp fighting there on September 14, 1862.

Chapter 7: The Aftermath of South Mountain

Chapter 7 explains the movements of the two armies to Sharpsburg and explains what happened at Antietam, as well as the importance and aftermath of that colossal battle.

The Battle of South Mountain: The History of the Civil War Battle that Led the Union and Confederate Armies to Antietam

Chapter 1: The Decision to Invade Maryland

After Robert E. Lee was installed as the commander of the Army of Northern Virginia during the Peninsula Campaign in June 1862, he quickly rallied the Confederate forces around Richmond and beat back George McClellan's Army of the Potomac later that month in a series of battles known as the Seven Days' Battles. As McClellan retreated up the peninsula, Lee reorganized the Army of Northern Virginia into the structure it is best remembered by. Stonewall Jackson now took command of a force consisting of his own division (now commanded by Brig. General Charles S. Winder) and those of Maj. General Richard S. Ewell, Brig. General William H. C. Whiting, and Maj. General D. H. Hill. The other wing of Lee's army was commanded by James Longstreet. On July 25, 1862, after the conclusion of the Seven Days Battles had brought the Peninsula Campaign to an end, JEB Stuart was promoted to Major General, his command upgraded to Cavalry Division.

Lee during the war

Stonewall Jackson

James Longstreet

JEB Stuart

Even before McClellan had completely withdrawn his troops, Lee sent Jackson's forces northward to intercept the new army Abraham Lincoln had placed under Maj. General John Pope, formed out of the scattered troops in the Virginia area. Pope had found success in the Western theater, and he was uncommonly brash, instructing the previously defeated men now under his command that his soldiers in the West were accustomed to seeing the backs of the enemy. Pope's arrogance turned off his own men, and it also caught the notice of Lee.

On June 26, General Pope deployed his forces in an arc across Northern Virginia; its right flank under Maj. General Franz Sigel positioned at Sperryville on the Blue Ridge Mountains, its center columns under Maj. General Nathaniel P. Banks at Little Washington, and its left flank under Maj. General Irvin McDowell at Falmouth on the Rappahannock River. On July 13, Lee responded by sending Jackson with 14,000 men to Gordonsville, with Maj. General A. P. Hill's division of 10,000 men set to join him by July 27.

Following the Battle of Cedar Mountain, General Jackson amassed his corps and marched (without opposition) to the Rappahannock River in eastern Virginia. Once certain McClellan was in full retreat, Lee joined Jackson, planning to strike Pope before McClellan's troops could arrive as reinforcements. In late August 1862, in a "daring and unorthodox" move, Lee divided his forces and sent Jackson northward to flank them, ultimately bringing Jackson directly behind Pope's army and supply base. This forced Pope to fall back to Manassas to protect his flank and maintain his lines of communication. Recognizing Lee's genius for military strategy, General Jackson quickly became Lee's most trusted commander, and he would later say that he so trusted Lee's military instincts that he would even follow him into battle blindfolded.

When Pope's army fell back to Manassas to confront Jackson, his wing of Lee's army dug in along a railroad trench and took a defensive stance. The Second Battle of Manassas or Bull Run was fought August 28-30, beginning with the Union army throwing itself at Jackson the first two days. When Longstreet's men finally arrived around noon on August 29, Lee informed Longstreet of his plan to attack the Union flank, which was at that time concentrating its efforts on General Jackson. Longstreet initially rejected Lee's suggestion to attack, recommending instead that a reconnaissance be conducted to survey the field. And although Longstreet's artillery was ultimately a major factor in helping Jackson resist the Union attack on August 29, his performance that day was described by some Lost Cause advocates as slow, and they considered his disobedience of General Lee insubordination. Lee's most famous biographer, Douglas Southall Freeman, later wrote: "The seeds of much of the disaster on July 2, 1863, at the Battle of Gettysburg were sown in that instant—when Lee yielded to Longstreet and Longstreet discovered that he would."

Nevertheless, the Second Battle of Bull Run or Manassas is considered one of Longstreet's most successful, While Jackson's men defended themselves the first two days, Lee used Longstreet's wing on August 30 to deliver a devastating flank attack before reinforcements from the retreating Army of the Potomac could reach the field. Longstreet's attack swept Pope's army off the field. Fought on the same ground as the First Battle of Manassas nearly a year earlier, the result was the same: a decisive Confederate victory that sent Union soldiers scrambling back to the safety of Washington.

After two days of fighting, Lee had achieved another major victory, and he now stood unopposed in the field 12 miles away from Washington, D.C. While Joseph Johnston and P.G.T. Beauregard had stayed in this position in the months after the First Battle of Bull Run, Lee determined upon a more aggressive course: taking the fight to the North.

In early September, convinced that the best way to defend Richmond was to divert attention to Washington, Lee decided to invade Maryland after obtaining Jefferson Davis's permission. On September 3, the famous general reported to the Confederate president:

HEADQUARTERS ALEXANDRIA AND LEESBURG ROAD,

Near Dranesville, September 3, 1862.

His Excellency President DAVIS,

Richmond, Va.:

Mr. PRESIDENT: The present seems to be the most propitious time since the commencement of the war for the Confederate Army to enter Maryland. The two grand armies of the United States that have been operating in Virginia, though now united, are much weakened and demoralized. Their new levies, of which I understand 60,000 men have already been posted in Washington, are not yet organized, and will take some time to prepare for the field. If it is ever desired to give material aid to Maryland and afford her an opportunity of throwing off the oppression to which she is now subject, this would seem the most favorable.

After the enemy had disappeared from the vicinity of Fairfax Court House, and taken the road to Alexandria and Washington, I did not think it would be advantageous to follow him farther. I had no intention of attacking him in his fortifications, and am not prepared to invest them. If I possessed the necessary munitions, I should be unable to supply provisions for the troops. I therefore determined, while threatening the approaches to Washington, to draw the troops into Loudoun, where forage and some provisions can be obtained, menace their possession of the Shenandoah Valley, and, if found practicable, to cross into Maryland. The purpose, if discovered, will have the effect of carrying the enemy north of the Potomac, and, if prevented, will not result in much evil.

The army is not properly equipped for an invasion of an enemy's territory. It lacks much of the material of war, is feeble in transportation, the animals being much reduced, and the men are poorly provided with clothes, and in thousands of instances are destitute of shoes. Still, we cannot afford to be idle, and though weaker than our opponents in men and military equipments, must endeavor to harass if we cannot destroy them. I am aware that the movement is attended with much risk, yet I do not consider success impossible, and shall endeavor to guard it from loss. As long as the army of the enemy are employed on this frontier I have no fears for the safety of Richmond, yet I earnestly recommend that advantage be taken of this period of comparative safety to place its defense, both by land and water, in the most perfect condition. A respectable force can be collected to defend its approaches by land, and the steamer Richmond, I hope, is now ready to clear the river of hostile vessels.

Should General Bragg find it impracticable to operate to advantage on his present frontier, his army, after leaving sufficient garrisons, could be advantageously employed in opposing the overwhelming numbers which it seems to be the intention of the enemy now to concentrate in Virginia.

I have already been told by prisoners that some of Buell's cavalry have been joined to General Pope's army, and have reason to believe that the whole of McClellan's, the larger portion of Burnside's and Cox's, and a portion of Hunter's, are united to it.

What occasions me most concern is the fear of getting out of ammunition. I beg you will instruct the Ordnance Department to spare no pains in manufacturing a sufficient amount of the best kind, and to be particular, in preparing that for the artillery, to provide three times as much of the long-range ammunition as of that for smooth-bore or short-range guns. The points to which I desire the ammunition to be forwarded will be made known to the Department in time. If the Quartermaster's Department can furnish any shoes, it would be the greatest relief. We have entered upon September, and the nights are becoming cool.

I have the honor to be, with high respect, your obedient servant,

R. E. LEE, General.

A few days later, Jefferson Davis responded to Lee's suggestion by approving an invasion of Maryland subject to a number of conditions:

General R. E. LEE, Commanding, &c.:

SIR: It is deemed proper that you should, in accordance with established usage, announce, by proclamation to the people of Maryland, the motives and purposes of your presence among them at the head of an invading army, and you are instructed in such proclamation to make known--

1st. That the Confederate Government is waging this war solely for self-defense; that it has no design of conquest, or any other purpose than to secure peace and the abandonment by the United States of their pretensions to govern a people who have never been their subjects, and who prefer self-government to a union with them.

2d. That this Government, at the very moment of its inauguration, sent commissioners to Washington to treat for a peaceful adjustment of all differences, but that these commissioners were not received, nor even allowed to communicate the object of their mission; and that, on a subsequent occasion, a communication from the President of the Confederacy to President Lincoln remained without answer, although a reply was promised by General Scott, into whose hands the communication was delivered.

3d. That among the pretexts urged for continuance of the war, is the assertion that the Confederate Government desires to deprive the United States of the free navigation of the Western rivers, although the truth is that the Confederate Congress, by public act, prior to the commencement of the war, enacted that "the peaceful navigation of the Mississippi River is hereby declared free to the citizens of any of the States upon its boundaries, or upon the borders of its navigable tributaries," a declaration to which this Government has always been, and is still, ready to adhere.

4th. That now, at a juncture when our arms have been successful, we restrict ourselves to the same just and moderate demand that we made at the darkest period of our reverses, the simple demand that the people of the United States should cease to war upon us, and permit us to pursue our own path to happiness, while they in peace pursue theirs.

5th. That we are debarred from the renewal of formal proposals for peace by having no reason to expect that they would be received with the respect mutually due by nations in their intercourse, whether in peace or in war.

6th. That, under these circumstances, we are driven to protect our own country by transferring the seat of war to that of an enemy, who pursues us with a relentless and, apparently, aimless hostility; that our fields have been laid waste, our people killed, many homes made desolate, and that rapine and murder have ravaged our frontiers; that the sacred right of self-defense demands that, if such a war is to continue, its consequences shall fall on those who persist in their refusal to make peace.

7th. That the Confederate army, therefore, comes to occupy the territory of their enemies, and to make it the theater of hostilities; that with the people themselves rests the power to put an end to this invasion of their homes, for, if unable to prevail on the Government of the United States to conclude a general peace, their own State government, in the exercise of its sovereignty, can secure immunity from the desolating effects of warfare on the soil of the State by a separate treaty of peace, which this Government will ever be ready to conclude on the most just and liberal basis.

8th. That the responsibility thus rests on the people of ------- continuing an unjust and oppressive warfare upon the Confederate States--a warfare which can never end in any other manner than that now proposed. With them is the option of preserving the blessings of peace by the simple abandonment of the design of subjugating a people over whom no right of dominion has ever been conferred, either by God or man.

In conjunction with giving Lee his approval, Davis wrote a public proclamation to the Southern people and, ostensibly, the Europeans whose recognition he hoped to gain. Recognizing the political sensitivity of appearing to invade the North instead of simply defending the home front, Davis cast the decision as one of self-defense, and that there was "no design of conquest", asserting, "We are driven to protect our own country by transferring the seat of war to that of an enemy who pursues us with a relentless and apparently aimless hostility."

Once he had his president's approval, Lee actually issued orders to be proclaimed before the citizens of Maryland, acutely aware that the border state had plenty of Confederate sympathizers who might not look kindly toward having their state invaded by the Confederate army:

TO THE PEOPLE OF MARYLAND:

It is right that you should know the purpose that has brought the army under my command within the limits of your State, so far as that purpose concerns yourselves.

The people of the Confederate States have long watched with the deepest sympathy the wrongs and outrages that have been inflicted upon the citizens of a Commonwealth allied to the States of the South by the strongest social, political, and commercial ties.

They have seen with profound indignation their sister-State deprived of every right and reduced to the condition of a conquered province.

Under the pretense of supporting the Constitution, but in violation of its most valuable provisions, your citizens have been arrested and imprisoned upon no charge and contrary to all forms of law; the faithful and manly protest against this outrage made by the venerable and illustrious Marylander to whom in better days no citizen appealed for right in vain was treated with scorn and contempt; the government of your chief city has been usurped by armed strangers; your legislature has been dissolved by the unlawful arrest of its members; freedom of the press and of speech has been suppressed; words have been declared offences by an arbitrary decree of the Federal executive, and citizens ordered to be tried by a military commission for what they may dare to speak.

Believing that the people of Maryland possessed a spirit too lofty to submit to such a government, the people of the South have long wished to aid you in throwing off this foreign yoke, to enable you again to enjoy the inalienable rights of freemen and restore independence and sovereignty to your State.

In obedience to this wish our army has come among you, and is prepared to assist you with the power of its arms in regaining the rights of which you have been despoiled.

This, citizens of Maryland, is our mission, so far as you are concerned. No constraint upon your free will is intended ; no intimidation will be allowed. Within the limits of this army at least, Marylanders shall once more enjoy their ancient freedom of thought and speech. We know no enemies among you, and will protect all, of every opinion. It is for you to decide your destiny freely and without constraint.

This army will respect your choice, whatever it may be; and, while the Southern people will rejoice to welcome you to your natural position among them, they will only welcome you when you come of your own free will.

Today the decision to invade Maryland is remembered through the prism of Lee hoping to win a major battle in the North that would bring about European recognition of the Confederacy, potential intervention, and possible capitulation by the North, whose anti-war Democrats were picking up political momentum. However, Lee also hoped that the fighting in Maryland would relieve Virginia's resources, especially the Shenandoah Valley, which served as the state's "breadbasket". And though largely forgotten today, Lee's move was controversial among his own men. Confederate soldiers, including Lee, took up arms to defend their homes, but now they were being asked to invade a Northern state. An untold number of Confederate soldiers refused to cross the Potomac River into Maryland.

Lee hinted at all of this in his report after the campaign while justifying his decision to make the invasion: "Although not properly equipped for invasion, lacking much of the material of war, and feeble in transportation, the troops poorly provided with clothing, and thousands of them destitute of shoes, it was yet believed to be strong enough to detain the enemy upon the northern frontier until the approach of winter should render his advance into Virginia difficult, if not impracticable. The condition of Maryland encouraged the belief that the presence of our army, however inferior to that of the enemy, would induce the Washington Government to retain all its available force to provide against contingencies, which its course toward the people of that State gave it reason to apprehend. At the same time it was hoped that military success might afford us an opportunity to aid the citizens of Maryland in any efforts they might be disposed to make to recover their liberties. The difficulties that surrounded them were fully appreciated, and we expected to derive more assistance in the attainment of our object from the just fears of the Washington."

For his part, General Longstreet also held the same view as Lee, believing an invasion of Maryland had plenty of advantages. He wrote of the decision in his memoirs, "The Army of Northern Virginia was afield without a foe. Its once grand adversary, discomfited under two commanders, had crept into cover of the bulwarks about the national capital. The commercial, social, and blood ties of Maryland inclined her people to the Southern cause. A little way north of the Potomac were inviting fields of food and supplies more plentiful than on the southern side; and the fields for march and manoeuvre, strategy and tactics, were even more inviting than the broad fields of grain and comfortable pasture-lands. Propitious also was the prospect of swelling our ranks by Maryland recruits."

Lee had also no doubt taken stock of the North's morale, both among its people and the soldiers of Pope's army and McClellan's army. In the summer of 1862, the Union had suffered more than 20,000 casualties, and Northern Democrats, who had been split into pro-war and anti-war factions from the beginning, increasingly began to question the war. As of September 1862, no progress had been made on Richmond; in fact, a Confederate army was now about to enter Maryland. And with the election of 1862 was approaching, Lincoln feared the Republicans might suffer losses in the Congressional midterms that would harm the war effort.

With all of that in mind, he restored General McClellan and removed General Pope after the second disaster at Bull Run. McClellan was still immensely popular among the Army of the Potomac, and with a mixture of men from his Army of the Potomac and Pope's Army of

Virginia, he began a cautious pursuit of Lee into Maryland.

Although McClellan had largely stayed out of the political fray through 1862, McClellan's most ardent supporters could not deny that he actively worked to delay reinforcing Pope during the Second Manassas campaign once the Army of the Potomac was evacuated from the Peninsula. Nevertheless, McClellan ultimately got what he wanted out of Pope's misfortune. Though there is some debate on the order of events that led to McClellan taking command, Lincoln ultimately restored McClellan to command, likely because McClellan was the only administrator who could reform the army quickly and efficiently.

McClellan

Naturally, McClellan's ascension to command of the armies around Washington outraged the Republicans in Congress and the Lincoln Administration, some of whom had all but branded him a traitor for his inactivity in early 1862 and his poor performance on the Peninsula. This would make it all the more ironic that McClellan's campaign into Maryland during the next few weeks would bring about the release of the Emancipation Proclamation.

Chapter 2: Initial Movements

The most fateful decision of the Maryland Campaign was made almost immediately, when early on Lee decided to divide his army into four parts across Maryland. Lee ordered Longstreet's men to Boonsboro and then to Hagerstown, Stonewall Jackson's forces to Harpers Ferry, and Stuart's cavalry and D.H. Hill's division to screen the Army of Northern Virginia's movements and cover its rear.

D.H. Hill

Why Lee chose to divide his army is still heavily debated among historians, who have pointed to factors like the importance of maintaining his supply lines through the Shenandoah Valley. Lee was also unaware what kind of resistance he might face at places like Frederick and Harpers Ferry, and it's also possible that he simply assumed McClellan's caution would allow him to take and keep the initiative and dictate the course of the campaign. With McClellan now assuming command of the Northern forces, Lee probably expected to have plenty of time to assemble his troops and bring his battle plan to fruition.

This time, however, McClellan was better prepared to face Lee. He had beaten Lee in a campaign through western Virginia in 1861 and had clearly underestimated Lee as a result during the Peninsula Campaign. Now, however, he realized that Lee was not the timid, indecisive general McClellan initially thought.

Though it was clear in early September that Lee had crossed the Potomac, the Army of

Northern Virginia decided to use ridges, mountains and cavalry to screen their movements. McClellan believed the most realistic goal was to drive the Confederates out of Maryland and aimed to do so, but his 85,000 strong Army of the Potomac moved conservatively into Maryland during the early portion of the campaign while still dealing with logistics. A report from the infamous intelligence chief Allan Pinkerton reached McClellan and estimated the rebel force at 100,000, while other reports couldn't ascertain the nature of the that army's movements or motives. McClellan told the Administration on September 10 that the estimates of the Army of Northern Virginia put it somewhere between 80,000-150,000 men, which obviously had a huge effect on the campaign.

THE LATE ALLAN PINKERTON.

Pinkerton

With the benefit of hindsight, historians now believe that Lee's entire Army of Northern Virginia had perhaps 50,000 men at most and possibly closer to 30,000 during the Maryland campaign. It's unclear how Lee's army, which numbered 55,000 before the Maryland Campaign, suffered such a steep drop in manpower, but historians have cited a number of factors, including disease and soldiers' refusal to invade the North. Lee clearly felt the pinch too, ordering his officers to keep straggling to a minimum and calling stragglers "unworthy members of an army that has immortalized itself". And far from Longstreet's hope that an invasion of Maryland would swell the Confederate ranks with sympathizers, it's estimated that only a few dozen at most latched on with the invading army in Maryland. Union general John Gibbon, who commanded the famed Iron Brigade during the campaign, also admitted his surprise with the people of Maryland, later writing, "I did not believe before coming here that there was so much Union feeling in the state. The whole population [of Frederick] seemed to turn out to welcome us. When Genl McClellan came thro the ladies nearly eat him up, they kissed his clothing, threw their arms around his horse's neck and committed all sorts of extravagances."

Gibbon

In his post-campaign report, Lee summarized the initial movements of his army leading up to September 12:

"It was decided to cross the Potomac east of the Blue Ridge, in order, by threatening Washington and Baltimore, to cause the enemy to withdraw from the south bank, where his presence endangered our communications and the safety of those engaged in the removal of our wounded and the captured property from the late battlefields. Having accomplished this result, it was proposed to move the army into Western Maryland, establish our communications with Richmond through the Valley of the Shenandoah, and, by threatening Pennsylvania, induce the enemy to follow, and thus draw him from his base of supplies.

It had been supposed that the advance upon Fredericktown would lead to the evacuation of Martinsburg and Harper's Ferry, thus opening the line of communication through the Valley. This not having occurred, it became necessary to dislodge the enemy from those positions before concentrating the army west of the mountains. To accomplish this with the least delay, General Jackson was directed to proceed with his command to Martinsburg, and, after driving the enemy from that place, to move down the south side of the Potomac upon Harper's Ferry. General McLaws, with his own and R. H. Anderson's division, was ordered to seize Maryland Heights, on the north side of the Potomac, opposite Harper's Ferry, and Brigadier-General Walker to take possession of Loudoun Heights, on the east side of the Shenandoa, where it unites with the Potomac. These several commands were directed, after reducing Harper's Ferry and clearing the Valley of the enemy, to join the rest of the army at Boonsborough or Hagerstown.

The march of these troops began on the 10th, and at the same time the remainder of Longstreet's command and the division of D. H. Hill crossed the South Mountain and moved toward Boonsborough. General Stuart, with the cavalry, remained east of the mountains, to observe the enemy and retard his advance.

A report having been received that a Federal force was approaching Hagerstown from the direction of Chambersburg, Longstreet continued his march to the former place, in order to secure the road leading thence to Williamsport, and also to prevent the removal of stores which were said to be in Hagerstown. He arrived at that place on the 11th, General Hill halting near Boonsborough to prevent the enemy at Harper's Ferry from escaping through Pleasant Valley, and at the same time to support the cavalry. The advance of the Federal Army was so slow at the time we left Fredericktown as to justify the belief that the reduction of Harper's Ferry would be accomplished and our troops concentrated before they would be called upon to meet it. In that event, it had not been intended to oppose its passage through the South Mountains, as it was desired to engage it as far as possible from its base.

General Jackson marched very rapidly, and, crossing the Potomac near Williamsport on the 11th, sent A. P. Hill's division directly to Martinsburg, and disposed the rest of his command to cut off the retreat of the enemy westward. On his approach, the Federal troops evacuated Martinsburg, retiring to Harper's Ferry on the night of the 11th, and Jackson entered the former place on the 12th, capturing some prisoners and abandoned stores."

On September 12, Stonewall Jackson's men were making their way to the outskirts of Harpers Ferry, whose garrison McClellan had unsuccessfully requested to have evacuated and added to his army. Meanwhile, the Union army was on the verge of entering Frederick, still unaware of Lee's dispositions but less than 20 miles behind the fragmented Confederate army.

It was around Frederick that the North was about to have one of the greatest strokes of luck during the Civil War. For reasons that are still unclear, Union troops in camp at Frederick came across a copy of Special Order 191, wrapped up among three cigars. The order contained Lee's entire marching plans for Maryland, making it clear that the Army of Northern Virginia had been divided into multiple parts, which, if faced by overpowering strength, could be entirely defeated in detail and bagged separately before they could gather back together into one fighting force. The Lost Order had been issued on September 9, and it read:

HDQRS. ARMY OF NORTHERN VIRGINIA,

September 9, 1862.

I. The citizens of Fredericktown being unwilling, while overrun by members of his army, to open their stores, in order to give them confidence, and to secure to officers and men purchasing supplies for benefit of this command, all officers and men of this army are strictly prohibited from visiting Fredericktown except on business, in which case they will bear evidence of this in writing from division commanders. The provost-marshal in Fredericktown will see that his guard rigidly enforces this order.

II. Major Taylor will proceed to Leesburg, Va., and arrange for transportation of the sick and those unable to walk to Winchester, securing the transportation of the country for this purpose. The route between this and Culpeper Court-House east of the mountains being unsafe will no longer be traveled. Those on the way to this army already across the river will move up promptly; all others will proceed to Winchester collectively and under command of officers, at which point, being the general depot of this army, its movements will be known and instructions given by commanding officer regulating further movements.

III. The army will resume its march tomorrow, taking the Hagerstown road. General Jackson's command will form the advance, and, after passing Middletown, with such portion as he may select, take the route toward Sharpsburg, cross the Potomac at the most convenient point, and by Friday morning take possession of the Baltimore and Ohio Railroad, capture such of them as may be at Martinsburg, and intercept such as may attempt to escape from Harper's Ferry.

IV. General Longstreet's command will pursue the main road as far as Boonsborough, where it will halt, with reserve, supply, and baggage trains of the army.

V. General McLaws, with his own division and that of General R. H. Anderson, will follow General Longstreet. On reaching Middletown will take the route to Harper's Ferry, and by Friday morning possess himself of the Maryland Heights and endeavor to capture the enemy at Harper's

Ferry and vicinity.

VI. General Walker, with his division, after accomplishing the object in which he is now engaged, will cross the Potomac at Cheek's Ford, ascend its right bank to Lovettsville, take possession of Loudoun Heights, if practicable, by Friday morning, Keys' Ford on his left, and the road between the end of the mountain and the Potomac on his right. He will, as far as practicable, co-operate with Generals McLaws and Jackson, and intercept retreat of the enemy.

VII. General D. H. Hill's division will form the rear guard of the army, pursuing the road taken by the main body. The reserve artillery, ordnance, and supply trains, &c., will precede General Hill.

VIII. General Stuart will detach a squadron of cavalry to accompany the commands of Generals Longstreet, Jackson, and McLaws, and, with the main body of the cavalry, will cover the route of the army, bringing up all stragglers that may have been left behind.

IX. The commands of Generals Jackson, McLaws, and Walker, after accomplishing the objects for which they have been detached, will join the main body of the army at Boonsborough or Hagerstown.

X. Each regiment on the march will habitually carry its axes in the regimental ordnance wagons, for use of the men at their encampments, to procure wood, &c.

By command of General R. E. Lee:

R. H. CHILTON,

Assistant Adjutant-General.

The "Lost Order" quickly made its way to General McClellan, who took several hours to debate whether or not it was intentional misinformation or actually real. McClellan is usually faulted for not acting quickly enough on these orders, but much of the instructions are vague and seemingly contradicted recent rebel movements. Moreover, McClellan was rightly concerned that the orders could be false misinformation meant to deceive the Union, since the manner in which the orders were lost was bizarre and could not be accounted for.

After about 18 hours, McClellan was confident enough that they were accurate and famously boasted to General Gibbon, "Here is a paper with which if I cannot whip Bobby Lee, I will be willing to go home." McClellan also wired Lincoln, "I have the whole rebel force in front of me, but I am confident, and no time shall be lost. I think Lee has made a gross mistake, and that he will be severely punished for it. I have all the plans of the rebels, and will catch them in their own trap if my men are equal to the emergency…Will send you trophies."

Though having Lee's marching plans offered McClellan an incredible advantage, the Lost Order may also have reinforced McClellan's belief that Lee's army had a significant advantage in manpower through its vague wording of "commands."

Chapter 3: Harpers Ferry

Harpers Ferry in the 1860s

As General Lee marched his Army of Northern Virginia down the Shenandoah Valley into Maryland, he planned to capture the garrison and arsenal at Harpers Ferry to secure his supply line back to Virginia. The Confederates were completely unaware of the Army of the Potomac's luck as they began to carry out Lee's plans, and Stonewall Jackson was already in the process of forcing the capitulation of Harpers Ferry.

To Stonewall Jackson's advantage, Col. Dixon S. Miles, Union commander at Harpers Ferry, had insisted on keeping most of his troops near the town instead of taking up commanding positions on the most important spot around the area: Maryland Heights. On September 12, Confederate forces engaged the Union's marginal defenses on the heights, but only a brief skirmish ensued. Then on September 13, two Confederate brigades arrived and easily drove the Union troops from the heights, even as critical positions to the west and south of town remained heavily defended.

On September 14, as the Army of the Potomac was bearing down on the Confederates around South Mountain several miles away, Jackson methodically positioned his artillery around Harpers Ferry and ordered Maj. Gen. A.P. Hill to move down the west bank of the Shenandoah River in preparation for a flank attack on the Union left the next morning. While Miles suggested surrendering, several officers among the garrison argued that they should attempt a breakout. When Miles suggested it was a "wild and impractical" idea, Benjamin "Grimes" Davis made clear that he would attempt it with men from the 12th Illinois Cavalry, the Loudoun Rangers, and other small units. Eventually, Davis successfully led about 1,400 men out of Harpers Ferry and inadvertently ran into the wagon train carrying Longstreet's ordnance. Porter Alexander, the chief artillerist of Longstreet's corps, explained, "My reserve ordnance train, of about 80 wagons, had accompanied Lee's headquarters to Hagerstown, and had also followed the march back to Boonsboro. I was now ordered to cross the Potomac at Williamsport, and go thence to Shepherdstown, where I should leave the train and come in person to Sharpsburg. The moon was rising as I started, and about daylight I forded the Potomac, unaware of having had a narrow escape from capture, with my train, by Gregg's brigade of cavalry. This brigade had escaped that night from Harper's Ferry, and crossed our line of retreat from Boonsboro. It had captured and destroyed the reserve ordnance train, of 45 wagons of Longstreet's corps."

By the following morning, September 15, Jackson had positioned nearly 50 guns on Maryland Heights and at the base of Loudoun Heights. Then he began a fierce artillery barrage from all sides, followed by a full-out infantry assault. Realizing the hopelessness of the situation, Col. Miles raised the white flag of surrender, enraging some of the men, one of whom beseeched him, "Colonel, don't surrender us. Don't you hear the signal guns? Our forces are near us. Let us cut our way out and join them." Miles dismissed the suggestion, insisting, "They will blow us out of this place in half an hour." Almost on cue, an exploding artillery shell mortally wounded Miles, and some historians have argued Miles was fragged by Union soldiers.

Jackson had lost less than 300 casualties while forcing the surrender of nearly 12,500 Union soldiers at Harpers Ferry, the largest number of Union soldiers to surrender at once during the entire war. For the rest of the day, the Confederates helped themselves to supplies in the garrison, including food, uniforms, and more, as Jackson sent a letter to Lee informing him of the success, "Through God's blessing, Harper's Ferry and its garrison are to be surrendered." Already a legend, Jackson earned the attention of the surrendered Union troops, who tried to catch a glimpse of him only to be surprised at his rather disheveled look. One of the men remarked, "Boys, he isn't much for looks, but if we'd had him we wouldn't have been caught in this trap."

As a result of the work to be done at Harpers Ferry, Jackson's men wouldn't be around to help Lee avoid a potential crisis at the various gaps in South Mountain. In fact, Jackson wouldn't even have all of his men at Sharpsburg in time to fight at Antietam on the 17th.

Chapter 4: Fox's Gap

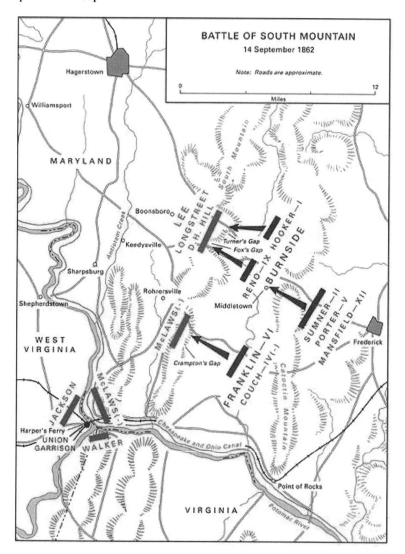

South Mountain on the 14th

It's unclear when Lee realized that McClellan had found a copy of his marching orders, and it's even possible that he knew almost right away. But that still gave Lee, who only had about 18,000 men at his disposal in the vicinity, little time to regroup. On the night of September 13 McClellan's army began moving at an uncharacteristically quick pace, and the following day, the advancing Union army began pushing in on the Confederate forces at several mountain passes at South Mountain: Crampton's Gap, Turner's Gap, and Fox's Gap. If McClellan's men could successfully push their way through these gaps, they would have an even greater chance of falling upon the different pieces of Lee's army. Lee explained this in his report to Jefferson Davis after the campaign: "Mr. PRESIDENT: My letter to you of the 13th instant informed you of the positions of the different divisions of this army. Learning that night that Harper's Ferry had not surrendered, and that the enemy was advancing more rapidly than was convenient from Fredericktown, I determined to return with Longstreet's command to the Blue Ridge, to strengthen D. H. Hill's and Stuart's divisions, engaged in holding the passes of the mountains, lest the enemy should fall upon McLaws' rear, drive him from the Maryland Heights, and thus relieve the garrison at Harper's Ferry."

There were two major points by which to cross South Mountain: Crampton's Gap and Turner's Gap. Crampton's was on the southwestern end of the mountain, while Turner's Gap was 12 miles to the north, with several small gaps in its near vicinity.[1] Orr's gap was located three miles to the north of Turner's and the Frosttown Gap was two miles south of Orr's. Less than one mile south of Turner's Gap was a mountain saddle known as Fox's Gap.

There were three primary roads (some were little more than foot paths) that ran through the gaps for crossing. The National Pike was the largest road in the region and crossed South Mountain at Turner's Gap. The Burkittsville-Rohrersville Road ran over Crampton's Gap while the Old Sharpsburg Road crossed the mountain at Fox's Gap. Running across the peak of the mountain perpendicular to these roads was Wood Road in the northern region with Ridge Road picking up south of Fox's Gap, where it continued south west until intersection with the Loop road, which lived up to its name and turned back east to link with the Old Sharpsburg road.[2] Due to the large number of routes around the mountain, there were but the three named above that actually crossed over the top. Because of the amount of access to the base and slopes, troop movement was necessary and rapid. This is something of which D.H. Hill was made aware when he was ordered from Boonsboro to protect the northern gaps.

On Sunday morning, September 14, 1862, General Stuart was reconnoitering with his cavalry when he and his men encountered two Federal brigades. The cavalry was pushed west, up into South Mountain. Alarmed, Stuart sent word to General D.H. Hill, who was headquartered in Boonsboro, that he needed a brigade of infantry dispatched to Turner's Gap to support his

[1] Richard Slotkin, *The Long Road to Antietam: How the Civil War Became a Revolution* (New York: W.W. Norton& Company, 2012), 193.
[2] Hoptak, 36-41.

cavalry in their endeavor to halt the Union advance. Hill was reluctant to disperse troops from Boonsboro since he was positioned there as a rearguard to prevent Union troops from escaping the Confederate forces at Harpers Ferry. He first sent General Alfred H. Colquitt's Brigade of Georgians to Turner's Gap. As further pleas came from Stuart, Hill in turn deployed Brigadier General Samuel Garland's Brigade, which was accompanied by Captain James W. Bondurant's Alabama Artillery and Captain John Lane's Georgia Battery.[3]

Through a series of miscommunications and discomfort within command, Lee ordered D.H. Hill to personally inspect the situation in the northern gaps and deploy his men accordingly for a proper defense.[4] Hill arrived at Turner's Gap at 5:30 in the morning, after which Stuart started south for Crampton's Gap with the remainder of his riders.

After surveying the situation, Hill ordered Brigadier General George B. Anderson to proceed from Boonsboro to Turner's Gap with his 1,200 men. Only the 4th Georgia regiment of Brigadier General Roswell Ripley's brigade was sent to Orr's Gap as Hill was reluctant to remove a large number of troops from Boonsboro.[5] While he was still on his reconnaissance, Hill mistook the voices of Colonel Thomas Rosser's 5th Virginia Cavalry for those of Union troops at Fox's Gap. Fearing the Federals were about to cross the mountain and disrupt Jackson's siege at Harper's Ferry, Hill immediately ordered Garland to march at the quick step south from Turner's Gap and to hold Fox's Gap "at all hazards."[6] Garland moved swiftly with two guns from Captain John Pelham's artillery in addition to the four guns of Bondurant's Alabama Artillery. After such a deployment of troops, D.H. Hill felt satisfied with his defenses as he held Garland in such high esteem that he once described him as "the most fearless man I ever knew."[7] Although Garland himself was a fearless and experiences leader, the five North Carolina regiments under his command were green troops and numbered just 1,100 strong.

At the opening of Fox's Gap was a clearing owned by farmer Daniel Wise. In a small corner of his field, he had a small cabin that became a landmark for Garland in positioning his troops. Although he was outnumber by the Union forces, Garland and the Confederates held the high ground, which in any battle is the greatest of advantages. The Federals were thus forced to climb the rocky slope on the east side of the mountain in order to attack at the crest thereby allowing the rebel artillery to rain down shell, canister, and grape at a deadly rate.

Garland had to stretch his rookie soldiers so as to cover all the passageways into the gap. North of the Wise cabin, on his left flank, he positioned the 20th North Carolina, with the 13th North Carolina next in the line of battle. Following south in line was Colonel Daniel Christie's

---

[3] Hoptak, 38-39.
[4] *OR*, series I, vol. 19, part I, 145.
[5] Hoptak, 39.
[6] Daniel Harvey Hill, "The Battle of South Mountain, or Boonsboro," in *Battles and Leaders of the Civil War*, vol. 2 (New York: The Century Company, 1887-1888), 562.
[7] *OR*, series I, vol. 19, part I, 1026.

23rd North Carolina regiment but because of the sparse number of troops, there was a gap of nearly 250 yards between the 23rd and 13th. Garland, in an attempt to lessen the gap, placed Bondurant's guns and men, known as the "Jeff Davis Artillery," in the space between these two infantry units. Further south along the line were the meager 90 men of the 12th North Carolina and finally on the far right of the line was the largest regiment, Colonel Duncan McRae's 400 man strong 5th North Carolina. To the right and front of the 5th were the two guns of Captain Pelham and covering the flank was Rosser's 5th Virginia Cavalry. This was a well-positioned, albeit lightly manned defensive position that was soon to face a portion of the Union Army's 9th Corps.

"It is probable that we shall have a serious engagement today & perhaps a general battle." General George McClellan wrote this is a note to his wife on Sunday morning, and the battle was taking shape in the early morning hours as troops from both armies were positioning themselves along the crest and base of South Mountain. The Kanawha Division of the 9th Corps, led by Brigadier General Jacob D. Cox, arose on the morning of the 14th at their camp five miles east of South Mountain. The day prior, Brigadier General Alfred Pleasonton, the Union cavalry commander, forced Stuart's Confederate horsemen to withdraw from Catoctin Valley, west toward South Mountain. Pleasonton was forced to halt his pursuit due to darkness and thus requested infantry support from Cox so as to resume the chase the following morning. On that morning, leading Cox's division on the march was Colonel Eliakim Scammon's brigade, which consisted of the 12th, 23rd, and 30the Ohio infantry regiments, the Western Virginia Cavalry, and Captain James McMullin's artillery battery. When they first broke camp, the troops thought they were embarking on a reconnaissance mission.

Pleasonton

While the Ohio troops marched westward to the base of South Mountain, General Pleasonton ordered an artillery barrage from the 10 long range guns he had positioned on the high ground in the nearby town of Bolivar. Lane's guns on the Confederate side responded and the sounds of battle had begun at approximately 9:00 that Sunday morning.

While his guns were attempting to pierce the Confederate defenses, Pleasonton presented his tactics to Colonel Scammon. He was to lead his Ohio troops straight along the Old Sharpsburg Road, aiming directly towards Fox's Gap. Once the gap was breeched, Scammon was to cut sharply north in order to capture the Confederate troops at Turner's Gap from the rear.

This was an aggressive if not lofty plan that left Scammon's men in great peril of assault from the rebel troops who held the high ground. The slopes of South Mountain were rocky and covered in dense brush, thereby making Scammon's ascent slow and arduous. Cox, aware of the cunning of the Confederate military leaders, warned all of Scammon's regimental commanders to "be prepared for anything, big or little- it might be a skirmish, it might be a battle."[8] It surely was a battle.

The musket balls began firing near 9:00 when Colonel Duncan McRae sent approximately 50 men of his 5th North Carolina regiment as skirmishers down the eastern slope of South Mountain. According to McRae's report, "They had not passed 50 steps from where we stood when they encountered the enemy's skirmishers and the fight commenced."[9] As McRae dispatched his skirmishers, so too did Lieutenant Colonel Rutherford B. Hayes, who was in command of the Union's 23rd Ohio regiment. The 23rd led Scammon's attack and was tasked with collapsing the Rebel's right flank and capturing their guns.[10] To the right of the 23rd in the battle line was Colonel Carr B. White's 12th Ohio, the regiment that found itself in the most precarious position at Fox's Gap. Whereas the 23rd had the grueling task of climbing the rocky slope with thick underbrush and copious amounts of forestry, White's 12th was forced to cross and climb over an open field with nothing to shield them from the raining shells and shots of Bondurant's guns. While these troops began their ascent, Colonel Hugh Ewing's 30th Ohio regiment was ordered to climb the slope directly in line with the gap. The Union advance was slow and mired due to heavy brush and rocky terrain, whereas the rebel soldiers were positioned on the high ground with a stone wall as a barrier.

---

[8] Jacob Dolson Cox, *Military Reminiscences of the Civil War,* 2 vols. (New York: Scribner's, 1900), 280.
[9] *OR,* series I, vol. 19, part I, 1040.
[10] Hoptak, 46.

Hayes

When the skirmish on the Union left began between the 23rd Ohio and 5th North Carolina, Confederate General Garland ordered McRae to move the entire 5th regiment forward in a full attack. This was difficult for McRae's men due to the heavily wooded landscape. According to McRae, the woods were so dense that, "it was impossible to advance in line of battle."[11] Hayes and his Ohio men faced the same dilemma on their climb. The environment was not conducive to a formal charge and Hayes was certain his battle line was on the verge of breaking, so he ordered a full bayonet charge. This was effective because McRae's inexperienced soldiers, many of who were in their first battle, fell back due to fright.

Hayes realized that the untried Confederates of the 5th North Carolina were in frightened disarray and quickly ordered another charge before the Rebel troops had time to reform their line. This was again successful as McRae's men fell back to their original position atop the mountain.[12] The equally green troops of the 12th North Carolina were so unnerved by Hayes' advance that they simply fired one round of musket balls and quickly scattered. It was only because of the reinforcement of the 23rd North Carolina that the Confederate line was able to be held.[13]

While the Ohio troops were hotly engaged in battle, General Cox called for reinforcements. He ordered the 2nd Brigade, under the command of Colonel George Crook, to support Scammon's men on the slope. Crook's brigade was also composed of three Ohio infantry regiments, the 11th, 28th, and 36th, in addition to Captain Frederick Schambeck's Chicago Dragoons and Captain Seth Simmonds Kentucky Light Artillery. All of this power totaled 1,500 men.[14] After sending a message to 9th Corps commander, General Reno, Cox galloped past Crook's men as they marched out of Middletown on their way to South Mountain.

While Crook's men were marching, Hayes' 23rd Ohio was still hotly engaged with the 23rd North Carolina. After the confusion of the retreat of the green soldiers, the 23rd North Carolina was able to halt the Ohio men's advance long enough for McRae to rally and reorganize his men. By doing so effectively, he was able to trap the 23rd Ohio in a crossfire. Hayes comprehended the situation and saw another bayonet charge as the only means by which to escape. However, before he was able to issue the order, Hayes took a musket ball to his arm and dropped to the ground. Hayes was gushing blood from the wound and "soon felt weak, faint, and sick at the stomach," yet was still able to maintain command of his troops. His men pulled him to the rear several feet and bound his wound. Hayes was in a position where he "could form a pretty accurate notion of the way the fighting was going," and he "could see wounded men staggering or carried to the rear."[15]

---

[11] *OR,* series I, vol. 19, part I, 1040-41.
[12] Hoptak, 47.
[13] *OR,* series I, vol. 19, part I, 1041.
[14] Cox, 280.
[15] Rutherford B. Hayes, *Diary and Letters of Rutherford B. Hayes: Nineteenth President of the United States* Vol.

While Hayes was being brought down the slope to safety, the 12th Ohio and subsequently the 30th were ordered to forge an attack up the mountain. As the 30th was engaged on the flank, the 12th was initially alone in pushing for the summit up the center. White's men were able to engage to such a degree that the Confederate command was forced to order Ruffin's 13th North Carolina and Iverson's 20th North Carolina south from their position at Wise's cabin in order to reinforce the center of his battle line. It was by this time that the 30th Ohio joined with the 12th. These combined forces were successful in reaching the summit and forced the rebel soldiers to fall back. This tremendous feat accomplished by the Ohio soldiers was completed amidst a cross-fire of artillery and musket shot. Upon reaching the summit, the Union soldiers fired so fiercely upon Bondurant's gunners that the artillery men were forced to fall back, but they took up a new position in the clearing at the gap.

As the Ohio troops were approaching the summit, Ruffin's 13th North Carolina regiment was closing from the Union right. White, commander of the 12th Ohio, recognized Ruffin's movement and ordered his men to turn and face the threat. Heavy fire erupted between the enemy regiments and it was not long before colonel Ruffin was shot in the hip and General Garland was blasted by a ball through his chest. Garland's wound was mortal and he died as his men were pulling him off the line. [16] McRae then assumed command of the brigade and continued to battle the Ohioans.

Although the Union soldiers had, in part, reached the summit, the Confederate line still held out. Bondurant's guns were now repositioned and poured shell and canister down on the Yankee soldiers. Ewing's men of the 30th Ohio were constantly under "a hail of grape" and were ordered to fall back.[17] On the crux of either a break through or retreat, Scammon asked that artillery be sent to push back the Rebel line and afford the Ohioans an opportunity to break through the gap.

At 11:00, Cox sent a couple of 10 pound guns under the direction of Lieutenant George Crome. It was soon after the guns became engaged that Crome was killed under the terrific fire of the 13th North Carolina. The guns and gunners were forced to withdraw, again leaving the Ohio infantry alone at the crest.

Around this time, Colonel Crook's men arrived with his 1,500 men. His 11th Ohio was able to join with the 23rd and then all were able to shift to the 12th Ohio's left. Crook's 36th filled the remaining hole between the 12th and the 30th and the men of the 28th fell in line behind the 30th. While Crook was positioning his men to advance, Confederate Colonel Charles Tew was positioning his 450 men of the 2nd and 4th North Carolina; these troops were a portion of Brigadier General George B. (G.B.) Anderson's brigade. As a result of confusing and faulty orders issued by Anderson, there was a space along the Confederate line that remained unfilled.

II, 1861-1865, edited by Charles Richard Williams (New York: Kraus Reprint Company, 1971), 356.
[16] Hoptak, 52.
[17] *OR,* series I, vol. 19, part I, 469.

The full Kanawha division took advantage of the cavity and commenced a brutal bayonet charge. McRae was astounded as he heard a "long extended yell," before the Union division, "bust upon our line."[18] Colonel White, commander of the 12th Ohio, reported," My regiment dashed over the crest and into a thicket of laurel under a severe fire. In this charge we drove the enemy in great confusion and inflicted serious loss upon him, killing several with the bayonet."[19]

After this massive charge by the Union infantry, the newly arrived men of the 2nd and 4th North Carolina were forced to scatter, leaving only Bondurant's guns and Ruffin's 13th North Carolina on Wise's field. Bondurant's artillerists did not hold out long as the 12th Ohio maneuvered to their rear and forced the gunners to retreat.

Now near noon, the only remaining Confederate force at the clearing of the gap was Ruffin's 13th North Carolina. Rather than surrender, Ruffin, who was completely surrounded by Union forces, was miraculously able to withdraw his men while fighting. He ordered a series of turns that confused the Union soldiers so much so that the men of the 13th North Carolina were able to safely withdraw.[20] With the Union now holding the summit, there was at last a lull in the fighting. The men from both armies rested on their arms as they remained relatively safe for near three hours.

Fearing a complete rupture of the line further down the western slope, General Longstreet ordered reinforcements to Fox's Gap. It was imperative for the Confederates to halt the Federals from any further advance, for if the Union Army pushed forward and severed the Rebel forces at Fox's Gap, Jackson's siege at Harpers Ferry would be in peril. The Confederates did not expect Miles and his garrison to withstand Jackson's assault for such a length of time; so they had to hold back Union forces at South Mountain if Jackson was to be successful. Thus, even though the fighting at Harpers Ferry is not considered part of the Battle of South Mountain, it was the primary reason the battle of the gaps was so fierce and desperate for both armies, and it was the reason General Longstreet ordered a counterattack at Fox's Gap.

Two brigades, under the commands of General Tige Anderson and General Thomas Drayton, met with D.H. Hill and were ordered to join with the remaining troops of G.B. Anderson and General Ripley. They were ordered south to forge the attack to remove the Federals from the summit at Fox's Gap. Ripley was to lead the men, totaling nearly 4,000, and form a strong line of battle. G.B. Anderson was positioned on the Confederate right with Ripley and Drayton in the center, thereby leaving Tige Anderson's men on the left flank. As a result of jumbled orders, Tige Anderson's unit marched too far south, thereby leaving an opening of 300 yards in the assault line.

Federal reinforcements were also pouring in at this time in anticipation of Longstreet's

[18] *OR,* series I, vol. 19, part I, 1042.
[19] *OR,* series I, vol. 19, part I, 464-65.
[20] Hoptak, 59.

planned counteroffensive. Brigadier General Orlando Bolivar Willcox of the 1st Division, IX Corps, ordered two brigades to Fox's Gap. The 1st Brigade under the command of Colonel Benjamin Christ, and the 2nd Brigade, led by Colonel Thomas Welsh, were composed of various regiments from Pennsylvania, Massachusetts, Michigan, and New York, and like their Confederate counterparts, many of these soldiers had not been battle tested. Private David Lane of the 17th Michigan noted, "Only two weeks from home, our uniforms were untarnished."[21] Lane's uniform was soon to be greatly tarnished as he and his fellow soldiers of the 17th Michigan faced off in battle against Confederate Colonel William Withington's 50th and 51st Georgia regiments. The Michigan troops were able to force the Georgians back and eventually coupled with the men of the 45th Pennsylvania, whose ranks were diminished by 136 (21 killed and 115 wounded) after their savage fight with Drayton's Rebel soldiers. Drayton's troops were positioned behind a stone wall and had the support of Bondurant's ever present gunners. Colonel Welsh, who was in command of the 45th Pennsylvania wrote, "Our troops continued to advance, utterly regardless of the slaughter in their ranks."[22]

Two additional units from the IX Corps, under the commands of Samuel Sturgis and Isaac Rodman, joined the fray, and the fighting was now at its peak. Major General Jess Reno rode to meet with Sturgis and survey the status of the battle with his own experiences eyes. As the sun was setting, McClellan called for a renewed attack as it seemed that the IX Corps had stalled in their advance. He received reports from his generals and proceeded to ride among his men to issue encouragement.

[21] David Lane, *A Soldier's Diary: The Story of a Volunteer, 1862-1865* (Jackson, MI, 1905), 11.
[22] *OR,* series I, vol. 19, part I, 440.

Reno

Reno was beloved by his troops and instilled the utmost confidence in the men in his service. As he was riding among his troops, noises were heard in the not too distance trees, thus prompting Reno to send skirmishers to investigate. Shortly after the scouts reached the woods, shots rang out and grew in intensity. The first volley of musket balls burst out of the thick foliage and struck Reno in the chest. His staff and soldiers moved quickly to transport him down the mountain for medical care, but to no avail; Jesse Reno, just 39 years of age, died soon after reaching the base of South Mountain. A member of the 48th Pennsylvania wrote in his journal that the "little General was well loved his loss was a great blow to the Ninth Corps."[23] As a result of Reno's death, Ambrose Burnside would lead the IX Corps at Antietam, and he played arguably the most controversial role in that battle, making Reno's loss even worse.

After the death of Reno, the fighting intensified until the combatants were no longer able

[23] Oliver Christian Bosbyshell, *The 48th in the War* (Philadelphia: Avil Printing Company, 1895), 76.

to see due to darkness. At the end of the day, the IX Corps held Fox's Gap and remained in the clearing of Wise's field, and by 10:00 that night, all Confederate troops were ordered way from Fox's Gap and were instructed to march the short distance north to Turner's Gap.

Through the almost 13 hours of fighting, the casualty toll was heavy. Aside from losing Corps commander Reno, the IX Corps suffered 889 casualties, 157 of which were killed in action. Confederate casualties are more difficult to determine because many war records were destroyed before the end of the war. It is reasonable to assert, however, that Garland and Drayton's units alone lost 40-50 percent of their troops, including Garland himself.[24]

These sad statistics represent just one-third of the fighting that took place on that day, because while the battle raged at Fox's Gap, ferocious fighting also took place just north at Turner's Gap.

Chapter 5: Turner's Gap

Later in his life, General D.H. Hill described Union Brigadier General George Meade as "one of our most dreaded foes."[25] Meade, best known today for commanding the Army of the Potomac against Lee at Gettysburg, proved worthy of this praise at South Mountain too as he led the 3rd Division of the I Corps up the slope of South Mountain. General Ambrose Burnside, who oversaw all operations of the I and IX Corps (thanks to McClellan's "Grand Division" organization of the army, which would prove unwieldy at Antietam) on September 14, 1862, ordered corps commander General Joseph Hooker to move his men north from Bolivar and strike the Confederate left flank at Turner's Gap. Hooker had three divisions with which to work, which consisted of 12,000 men in addition to nine artillery batteries. The 1st Division was commanded by Brigadier General John Hatch, the 2nd by Brigadier General James Ricketts, and Meade controlled the 3rd. He and his troops were camped approximately two miles outside of Frederick on the night of September 13 and were given the order to march the following morning.

They left Frederick and passed over Catoctin Mountain and across the Middletown Valley. Hooker's strategy for his I Corps was to march the infantry west across the valley into Bolivar then to proceed north then quickly again west directly into the mountain. Meanwhile, one mile north of Bolivar on a high ground near Mount Tabor Church, Hooker positioned Captain John Cooper's Battery B, 1st Pennsylvania Light Artillery, which consisted of four three-inch rifles.[26]

---

[24] Hoptak, 85.
[25] Hill, "The Battle of South Mountain," 574.
[26] Ethan Rafuse, *Antietam, South Mountain, & Harpers Ferry: A Battlefield Guide* (Lincoln: University of Nebraska Press, 2008), 187-88.

Meade

Once his troops had gained the northern position Hooker planned, Meade and Hatch's troops were to attack separately yet simultaneously. There were two outcroppings north of Turner's Gap that were being lightly held by Confederate forces. The northern spur was to be attacked by Meade while Hatch was to assault the ridge just to the south. Rickett's 2nd Division was held in reserve to reinforce when needed. Hooker ordered the advance to begin at five o'clock that afternoon, thus Meade began positioning his troops to assault the north spur. He deployed Colonel Albert Lewis Magilton's three Pennsylvania regiments, the 4th, 7th, and 8th, on the left end of the battle line. In the center he placed Colonel Thomas Foster Gallagher's 9th, 10th, 11th, and 12th regiments. To Gallagher's right were five Pennsylvania reserve regiments under the command of Brigadier General Truman Seymour.

Defending against this great force was problematic for General D.H. Hill. To protect both the north and south spurs, Hill had at his disposal less than 1,800 men, and Meade was attacking the Confederates with more than 4,000 troops. Brigadier General Robert Rodes had his 1,200 Alabama troops spread out across the span of both spurs and was to receive support only from the less than 600 South Carolinians under the command of Colonel Peter F. Stevens.[27] From above, Hill and Rodes watched the Federal troops amass at the bottom of the eastern slope of South Mountain. Not only were these soldiers aware that Meade's troops outnumbered them greatly, they were also aware that the Confederate line on their right at Fox's Gap was collapsing. Because of the route of the Zittlestown road, which ran to the left of Rodes on the north spur and continued around behind his line, both he and Hill understood that if Hooker was able to turn the left of the battle line, Rodes and his men would surely be taken. Hill became increasingly concerned and ordered Rodes to move his entire brigade up to the north spur. Rodes of course complied with these orders, but by doing so an opening of almost one mile in his battle line resulted. Additionally, by moving his men north, Rodes left the artillery alone without infantry protection on the south spur. In order to rectify this tactical miscue, Rodes ordered Colonel Bristol Gayle to turn his 12th Alabama infantry regiment back to the south spur. This left General Rodes with only four Alabama regiments   as Stevens had yet to arrive with his South Carolina troops   to defend against the Union advance. His line of battle had Colonel E. O'Neal's 26th Alabama holding the right flank with Colonel Cullen Battle's 3rd Alabama on his left. Next was the 5th Alabama regiment under the command of Major Edwin Lafayette Hobson. Holding the left flank, perhaps the most precarious of the Confederate positions, was Colonel John Gordon and his 6th Alabama infantry. The distance from Gordon's left down to Gayle's right on the south spur was nearly 4,000 feet. Compounding the predicament was the fact that, due to the ravines and landscape in general, all of these troops were situated in such a manner that contact and communication between them was all but impossible.

Finally, at approximately 4:00 in the afternoon, the South Carolina Brigade arrived to lend support in defense of Turner's Gap. Another two brigades under the leadership of General John Bell Hood were also present but were quickly sent south in an attempt to hold the crumbling line at Fox's Gap while Stevens and his men were immediately dispatched north to Turner's Gap in order to bolster the defenses of General Rodes. Stevens was leading his troops in that direction when, through a mishap in the chain of command, he received conflicting orders and therefore halted his troops. While waiting for clarification, he grew increasingly aware that the Yankee soldiers were gaining ground and feared he would not be able to hold his position. He had his men close by the Dahlgren road and deployed them on the spot. To the left of the passage he placed the 18th, 22nd, and 23rd South Carolina while on the opposite side of the road stood only

---

[27] Hill, 573.

the 17th South Carolina. In total, Stevens had the strength of 550 infantry troops positioned alongside Dahlgren Road, which left Rodes alone with his 1,200 men atop the spurs to face off against the 4,000 men under Meade's command who were rapidly approaching.[28]

By the time the soldiers in blue began their ascent, Confederate skirmishers had already been sent from the spurs to scout the region. Colonel Gayle dispatched forty of his 12th Alabama men under the leadership of Lieutenant Robert E. Park to probe the dense area. Park's men spotted Meade's battle lines just to the rear of a skirmish party composed of riflemen from the 13th Pennsylvania Reserves. This regiment, also known as the 1st Pennsylvania Rifles, was commonly referred to as the "Bucktails," due to the deer tails they donned on their caps. After spying the Bucktails, Park "concealed my men behind trees, rocks and bushes and cautioned them to aim well before firing."[29] As Colonel Hugh McNeil led his Bucktails across the rocky terrain, they were observed by the Confederate artillerists positioned on the south spur. The perfectly accurate guns blistered the Bucktails from the spur. Seymour reported that "numbers fell under the accurate fire of the shells."[30]

Before these Pennsylvania riflemen grasped the situation, Park's hidden skirmishers opened fire on the already reeling Yankees. Those who were able, instantly found cover behind any object and began to take aim at the rebel shooters. Once the Bucktails started firing, Park's men fell in droves. Whereas the Confederate soldiers were primarily firing with muskets, the Pennsylvania Bucktails had the advantage of the far more accurate Sharp rifle. The Union army had access to the arsenal in Springfield, Massachusetts, and until that day in September, the one in Harpers Ferry, so arming their men with the latest and most accurate weapons was done with ease. The Confederate soldiers, most of whom were forced to supply their own weapons, were by-and-large forced to fight against rifles with only their inaccurate muskets. Bravely; however, Park's skirmishers were able to delay the Federal advance until Seymour ordered in an additional regiment, the 2nd Pennsylvania Reserves.

The one advantage possessed by the Confederate forces was their position on the high ground. The terrain was not only forested, rocky, and dense over which the Union troops were forced to cross, there were also many structures along the path up the mountain. There were scattered small homes and barns in addition to several other out buildings. This was a conundrum for the Federals, as they were certain rebel soldiers were hiding in the buildings ready to take aim, but unfortunately for Seymour's Pennsylvanians, coming into contact with these buildings was necessary if they were to capture the north spur. Both Seymour and his foe Rodes were keenly aware that this rocky outcrop to the north of Turner's Gap was to be the key point of battle. If the Union took that ground, Rodes and his Alabamians would be flanked and forced to retreat. In the hopes of avoiding this, Rodes deployed the 6th Alabama regiment further north to

---

[28] OR, series I, vol. 19, part I, 941.
[29] Park quoted in Hill, 572.
[30] OR, series I, vol. 19, part I, 272.

defend the north spur. It was imperative to the Confederate defense that Seymour not be allowed to penetrate the line at that point, for if they did, the Yankees would then forge their way behind Rodes and have an unobstructed march to Turner's Gap. Seymour acted swiftly in ordering the Pennsylvania Reserves to charge, but was fairly too late as Gordon's 6th Alabama had already positioned themselves further north and began assaulting the Union soldiers with musket balls.[31]

As the fighting drew on, Seymour sent even more troops to flank Gordon on the left while at once he ordered Colonel Joseph Fisher to mount an attack on Gordon's right. The grossly outmanned Confederate soldiers somehow managed to maintain their position and held off the Federal assault on both sides of Gordon's line. Frustrated by this apparent standstill, Captain Edwin Irvin, commander of the Bucktails' Company K, took it upon himself to charge straight up the center of the line. He was instantly shot in the head, but this inspired act motivated his comrades and Irvin's fellow Bucktails made a full charge and managed to flank Gordon on the left. Gordon realized his situation was hopelessly untenable and ordered a retreat.[32]

Unbeknownst to Seymour as he halted his men on the cleared north spur, Major Hobson's 5th Alabama was concealed behind a stone wall near the edge of a cornfield. Seymour's men were immediately fired upon, which infuriated the stunned Seymour. Reportedly, Seymour turned to Fisher with the order, "Colonel, put your regiment into that cornfield and hurt somebody!" Accordingly, Fisher replied, "I will, general, and I'll catch one alive for you."[33] Fisher was as good as his word, flushing out the Alabamians and taking 11 as prisoners while the rest scattered. Once the cornfield was cleared, the Union forces held the left portion of the north spur and controlled the strategically important Zittlestown Road.

Concurrently, Colonels Magilton and Gallagher were combatting the three remaining Alabama regiments on the right. Colonel Magilton, on the left of the battle line, was aimed directly at Stevens' men who were desperately trying to safely escape their position along Dahlgren Road in order to link up with Rodes. To the Federal right was Gallagher's force, which stood to face the remainder of the Alabama regiments. In the center of Gallagher's line was the 11th Pennsylvania Reserves regiment, commanded by Lieutenant Colonel Samuel M. Jackson. They were located in the unenviable position between the spurs and near a deep mountain gorge, wherein they began receiving a short range volley from the 3rd Alabama. To their right was the 9th Pennsylvania under the leadership of Lieutenant Colonel Robert Anderson.

The men of the Keystone State were momentarily halted by the skirmishing activity of the 3rd Alabama. These rebels were cleverly concealed within a small house owned by a family named Haupt. Seeing no other option, Anderson ordered his men to begin peppering the Haupt home with hot firing. On the left of the Federal advance was the 12th Pennsylvania regiment, who

---

[31] Hoptak, 99-100.
[32] Hoptak, 100.
[33] J.R. Syphert, *History of the Pennsylvania Reserve Corps* (Lancaster, PA: Elias Barr, 1865), 369-370.

encountered little to no resistance from the fleeing 26th Alabama. During the melee of battle, Colonel Gallagher was shot in the arm and turned over command of the 3rd Brigade to the 9th's Lieutenant Colonel Anderson, who in turn placed Captain Samuel Dick in charge of his regiment. As the men of the 9th were nearly exhausted of ammunition, Captain Dick ordered a full bayonet charge, which was successful in finally driving the Alabamians from the Haupt house. The wounded Anderson watched his troops with pride and reported, "Our line moved steadily on, not once giving way or faltering."[34]

The 9th regiment, at this point nearly deplete of ammunition, was relieved by their fellow Pennsylvanians of the 10th infantry. In the center of the line, the 11th Pennsylvania was at last able to dislodge "the enemy [3rd Alabama] from their strong and well-selected position."[35] It was at this time, nearing a late summer sunset, that Colonel Stevens at last arrived with his South Carolina troops. When all was thought lost, Rodes was rejuvenated at the sight of Stevens and rallied the remainder of his troops to the peak of the spur. Along with Steven's South Carolina regiment were the remnants of the 6th, 3rd, and 12th Alabama. Rodes created an ersatz line of battle and engaged in close range fighting with Anderson's men at their front and Seymour's troops who were still advancing from the left. The heated contest was brief, and when darkness had fallen, Rodes men had retreated 200 yards north of Turner's Gap.

Rodes lost nearly one-third of his gallant brigade. 204 were missing, 157 were wounded, and the killed numbered 61, including Colonel Gayle. The 1st Pennsylvania was engaged with Gayle's men and the commander reported that with "darkness coming on, we were unable to pursue the enemy further, and lay on our arms for the night." The report continues by mentioning the death of Gayle and that his "body was carefully buried by my men."[36] Meade's Pennsylvanians succeeded in taking the north spur from the Confederate defense, but they suffered 392 casualties: 95 killed, 296 wounded, and only one missing.

Meanwhile, on the south spur Brigadier General John Hatch, commander of the I Corps' 1st Division deployed his three brigades in three lines of battle. The forward line was commanded by Brigadier General Marsena Patrick. Following 200 yards to his rear was Colonel Walter Phelps Jr.'s brigade with Brigadier General Abner Doubleday and his troops an equal distance behind Phelps. In total, Hatch advanced 2,400 troops simultaneously with the march of Meade's men on the north spur at 5:00 p.m.

[34] *OR*, series I, vol. 19, part I, 275.
[35] *OR*, series I, vol. 51, part I, 153.
[36] *OR*, series I, vol. 51, part I, 142.

Hatch

Patrick sent two New York regiments ahead as skirmishers to probe the enemy and elicited but few harmless artillery bursts from the lone rebel guns. The Confederates were in desperate need of reinforcements and they came in the form of some exhausted troops. Brigadier Generals James Kemper and Richard Garnett marched their Virginians to the south spur from 15 miles away. Also starting in Hagerstown that morning was Colonel Joseph Walker's South Carolina force. These men were on a forced march at the quick step and endured an endless stream of dirt and dust along with high temperatures and little water. Initially, these troops were ordered further south to Fox's Gap before the order was reversed and they were forced to about face and march back north to the south spur of Turner's- Gap. Garnett, who wrote "my troops were almost exhausted," estimated that his men marched 18-20 miles in the heat and without rest before they even engaged in battle. [37] Longstreet was taken aback by their appearance and later noted that the newly arrived troops were "thinned to skeletons."[38]

LONG MARCH FROM HAGGSTOWN

---

[37] *OR,* series I, vol. 19, part I, 894-95.

[38] James Longstreet, *From Manassas to Appomattox: Memoirs of the Civil War in America* (Philadelphia: J.B. Lippincott Co., 1896), 226.

These men were an inferior opponent in their condition for the large force of the Union Army. Although the Federal advance was halted because Patrick's battle line had thinned and separated due to the terrain, the bayonet charge ordered by Phelps resulted in the Yankee soldiers reaching and surmounting the stone wall behind which Garnett's men were position and forcing the Confederate to withdraw. There was continued fighting on the south spur after darkness had fallen. Some of Garnett's troops reformed with Colonel Walker's South Carolina soldiers. This makeshift unit put forth an inspired, and at times wild, effort, but they were unable to drive the Federal troops from the spur. While the Union suffered 180 casualties, Garnett lost nearly 50 percent of his force.

The fighters of the north were so far successful in capturing both the north and south spurs. It was Turner's Gap itself; however, that was strongly in Confederate possession. John Gibbon's brigade had been dispatched to Bolivar by General Burnside on the morning of September 14. Confederate General Colquitt held a strong position on the high ground directly to the east of Turner's Gap. Burnside ordered Gibbon to march along the National Pike and attack directly to the front of Colquitt in order to take the gap. On the north side of the turnpike, Colquitt positioned the 600 men of the 23rd and 28th Georgia regiments while on the other side of the road he had a force of 700 men in the regiments of the 13th Alabama, 27th, and 6th Georgia, for a total of 1,300 troops.

Advancing against the Confederates was the Black Hat Brigade, comprised of Western regiments from Wisconsin and Indiana. They had first seen battle just weeks ago against the Stonewall Brigade at Brawner's Farm during the Second Bull Run campaign, but they would earn the eternal nickname Iron Brigade for attacking uphill against the Confederates.

The Black Hat Brigade under Gibbon waited patiently until nightfall on September 14 before they were deployed into action at Turner's Gap with the rest of Hooker's I Corps. The four regiments straddled the National Road as they pushed toward Turner's Gap. Captain John Callis's 7th Wisconsin led the brigade on the right, with Colonel Edward Bragg's 6th just behind them to the right, and Colonel Solomon Meredith's 19th Indiana took position on the left, with Colonel Lucius Fairchild's 2nd Wisconsin just behind them.[39] As they made their way into the fight, Rufus Dawes of the 6th Wisconsin recalled that "long lines and heavy columns of dark blue infantry could be seen pressing up the green slopes of the mountain, their bayonets flashing like silver in the ray of the setting sun, and their banners waving in beautiful relief against the background of green."[40]

The Black Hat Brigade met Colonel A.H. Colquitt's brigade of five Alabama and Georgia regiments along the National Road as they fought their way up the mountain to Turner's Gap. The Union army moved slowly and carefully into the mountain passes, hoping to overwhelm

---

[39] Nolan, *The Iron Brigade*, 122-123.
[40] Dawes, *A Full Blown Yankee of the Iron Brigade*, 80.

Confederate forces. Darkness fell on the soldiers of the Black Hat Brigade as they made their way up the mountain, but they pushed on. The Confederates were better hidden in the cover of the mountain, and were therefore able to bombard Hooker's I Corps with great success, but the I Corps continued to push forward into the mountain as the night wore on.

At the height of the battle, Colwell's skirmishers in the 2nd Wisconsin came under rapid attack by Hill's troops, hidden in a house up the side of the mountain. Meredith quickly deployed the 19th Indiana to aid the 2nd Wisconsin, flushing out the Confederates on the left flank. At the same time, Meredith ordered the artillery to thrash the house, and dozens of Confederate soldiers emerged, giving the 19th Indiana a temporary upper hand in the fight.[41] The remaining concealed Confederate troops continued exchanging fire with the 2nd Wisconsin and 19th Indiana as they slowly pushed through the mountain pass. In the meantime, the 6th and 7th Wisconsin had been considerably more successful, pushing Confederate troops much further through the pass, until they came upon an open field and found themselves surrounded by the enemy. The 6th and 7th Wisconsin defended themselves admirably, exchanging fire with the enemy for hours and coming to a stalemate as the light of morning approached. At times, the troops of the two opposing sides were so close they could shout insults to one another.

Finally, the 2nd Wisconsin and 19th Indiana joined them, driving off Confederate reinforcements and especially the 23rd Georgia's brutal skirmishers. While the Confederate forces received somewhat steady reinforcements, the Western regiments had only each other to get through the long night of fighting.[42]

When Gibbon heard that Hooker and Reno had successfully fought off the Confederates at the other positions on South Mountain, he ordered his regiments to cease fire, thinking the larger battle had been won. They had at least managed to secure the mountain crest, successfully weakening the Confederates' position at Turner's Gap. Nevertheless, the Confederates took advantage of the temporary lull and attacked the Federals once again. The 7th Wisconsin charged back at them with fixed bayonets, breaking the Confederate line and forcing them to retreat in confusion. Both sides soon ran out of ammunition and ceased fire once again, so that the troops could finally take a much-needed rest.

By dusk, the Confederates were on the verge of losing Turner's Gap and Fox's Gap. Amidst rumors of the Confederate withdrawal early the next morning, the 6th Wisconsin sent into the darkness three cheers for the "Badger State" without a response from the enemy, confirming their victory. It was a costly victory, however, as they had lost a quarter of their forces, with 37 killed, 251 wounded, and 30 missing in action, compared to a Confederate loss of just over 100.[43]

The Battle of South Mountain had been "terrible work," McClellan noted, but the Black Hat

---

[41] Nolan, *The Iron Brigade,* 126-127.
[42] Nolan, *The Iron Brigade,* 128-130.
[43] Nolan, *The Iron Brigade,* 127-128.

Brigade in particular had distinguished itself, and General Gibbon had "handled his brigade with as much precision and coolness as if upon a parade, and the bravery of his troops could not be excelled."[44] McClellan and Burnside, along with several other officers, had witnessed the advance of Gibbon's brigade up the mountainside, marveling at what appeared to be continued progress against steady enemy fire, in what Burnside called "a most brilliant engagement."[45]

It was during this observation of the fighting on the road up South Mountain that General McClellan was said to have given Gibbon's brigade its famous nickname. McClellan asked General Hooker about the men fighting along the pike, and when Hooker told him that they were General Gibbon's brigade of Western men, McClellan replied, "They must be made of iron." Hooker replied, "By the eternal, they are iron. If you had seen them at Bull Run as I did you would know them to be of iron." McClellan acknowledged, "Why General Hooker, they fight equal to the best troops in the world."[46] Thus, in the shadow of South Mountain, was born the Iron Brigade of the West, but while they may have just earned their name, they wouldn't have long to recover.

In his official report on the action at Turner's Gap, Colquitt stated, "Not an inch of ground was yielded."[47]Gibbon's wounded and dying men were forced to remain on the slope for the night because in the darkness, and on such unforgiving terrain, stretcher bearers were unable to traverse the landscape. Dawes recalled that the fallen were "scattered over a great distance up and down the mountain, and were suffering untold agonies…dying men were pleading piteously for water, of which there was not a drop in the regiment." As he scanned his surroundings, Dawes witnessed the "dread reality of war."[48]

Several miles to the south of Dawes, that same reality was taking place at Crampton's Gap.

Chapter 6: Crampton's Gap

As it turned out, the crucial pass held by Confederate forces on South Mountain was Crampton's Gap. This crossing was nearly six miles to the south of where the fighting took place at Fox's and Turner's Gaps. If the Union Army was able to penetrate the Confederate line at this juncture, Confederate General McLaws' line would have been compromised from the rear. McLaws had a portion of his troops stationed on Maryland Heights overlooking Harpers Ferry to bolster General Jackson's assault on that Federal garrison. The remainder of McLaws' forces were stationed near Crampton's Gap on the southern portion of the mountain. If done expeditiously,

[44] Jean Huets, "The Iron Brigade."
[45] Nolan, *The Iron Brigade,* 127-128.
[46] Quoted in Cullen B. Aubrey, *Recollections of a newsboy in the Army of the Potomac, 1861-1865. His capture and confinement in Libby Prison, after being paroled, sharing the fortunes of the famous Iron Brigade* (Milwaukee, 1904), 19.
[47] *OR*, series I, vol. 19, part I, 1053.
[48] Dawes, 84.

the capture of this gap meant that the Yankee soldiers might be able to reach Colonel Miles at Harpers Ferry before his troops were overrun.

For this significant mission, General McClellan assigned Major General William B. Franklin's VI Corps. McClellan issued his subordinate specific orders and clearly explained his strategic goals. Franklin was instructed to "move at daybreak in the morning by Jefferson and Burkittsville," as the crossing was to be on the south end of the mountain, either at Crampton's, or the smaller Brownsville Gap, less than one mile to the south. McClellan's ultimate goal was for Franklin to secure the gap quickly, then without haste, proceed into Rohrersville to halt the Rebel retreat and destroy McLaws' troops from the rear. McClellan had notions of Franklin rescuing Miles from his predicament at Harpers Ferry and subsequently have those troops join with Franklins to either assist Burnside's men at Turner's Gap or to "take the road from Rohrersville to Sharpsburg & Williamsport in order either to cut off the retreat of Hill and Longstreet towards the Potomac, or to prevent the repassage of Jackson."[49]

The ambitious plan was sound but was poorly executed by Franklin. Franklin's VI Corps broke camp in Buckeyestown, a mere four miles from Jefferson, at life-thirty on the morning of September, 14. Franklin had a full two divisions under his command, the 1st commanded by Major General Henry W. Slocum, and the 2nd under the leadership of Major General William Farrar Smith. Each division was comprised of three brigades yet only General William T.H. Brook's Vermont soldiers saw action that day. The remaining two brigades, under the leadership of Generals Winfield Scott Hancock and William Irwin, sat in reserve. The 1st Division faced the brunt of the battle. Colonels Joseph J. Bartlett and Alfred T.A. Torbert, along with Brigadier General John Newton led their troops of the 1st Division into fierce battle. In total, Franklin's numbers neared 13,000 while the Confederates had less than 2,500 men who participated that day.

---

[49] *OR,* series I, vol. 19, part I, 45-46.

Franklin

The Southern troops were not only sparse in number but also at a disadvantage in that they did not know from which gap the Federals would come. Confederate General Paul Semmes, who commanded a brigade of Georgia and Virginia soldiers, predicted Franklin's troops would aim for Brownsville Pass but still had to protect Crampton's as a precaution. He remained at Brownsville with the 53rd Georgia, 15th and 32nd Virginia regiments, and Captain Basil Manley's Battery A, 1st North Carolina Light Artillery. He held the 10th Georgia infantry in Pleasant Valley, between South Mountain and Harpers Ferry, and deploy them as necessary. Colonel William Allen Parham was stationed with his 6th, 12th, and 16th Virginia infantry regiments at Crampton's Gap. Supporting Parham was Colonel Thomas Munford's small band of 275 horsemen, which consisted of the 2nd and 12th Virginia Cavalry.[50]

Parham deployed his men along the Mountain Church Road, which ran parallel to South Mountain at its base on the eastern slope. On either flank he had the dismounted men of Munford's Cavalry; the 12th on the left and the 2nd protecting the right. His infantry troops were spread so thin across the middle of the road that in some instances eight to ten feet separated one soldier from another. The 12th Virginia was positioned in the center of the line with the 16th on

---

[50] Hoptak, 135-36.

their left and the 6th to their right. Parham and Munford's force at Crampton's Gap totaled just 800 men. While Semmes maintained control of just 300 additional soldiers at Brownsville Pass.[51]

As the rebel soldiers made their way up the western slope to form at the southern gaps, Franklin's VI Corps was also becoming organized. The evening prior to the attack on the gaps, General McClellan informed Franklin that his two divisions were to lead the assault and were to be joined when possible by General Couch's 4th Division. He also explicitly ordered Franklin not to wait for Couch at any juncture of his march. These orders went unheeded by Franklin and as a result he lost precious time that allowed the Confederate forces to strengthen their numbers. Once their march was underway from Buckeyesville, scouts from the 6th Pennsylvania Cavalry encountered pickets from Munford's 2nd Virginia riders. A message was sent to the commander of the 96th Pennsylvania infantry regiment, Colonel Henry Cake, that assistance was needed in the advance. Cake dispatched two companies of skirmishers who were able to approach part of the Rebel main line. The 96th engaged the Confederates in a large skirmish that lasted nearly three hours. While at the same time, Franklin and the remainder of the corps reached Burkittsville. The commander ordered artillery to be positioned on the high ground just to the east of the town and three batteries were dispatched. Incredibly, Franklin decided to take a one hour rest in Burkittsville in order to eat lunch and smoke cigars. This act was in direct contrast of McClellan's order to move as expeditiously as possible. This inexplicable action afforded the Confederates, who were at once looking down upon the entire corps from the slope of the mountain, time to reinforce yet again.

When McLaws saw the Federal forces amassing below, he ordered Brigadier General Howell Cobb to march his men as quickly as possible to Brownsville Pass and wait for instructions as to which crossing his men were to defend. Without confusion, McLaws instructed Cobb to "hold the gap even if he lost his last man doing it."[52] Concurrently, Semmes ordered additional guns to be deployed to Brownsville and ordered the waiting 10th Georgia to Crampton's Gap to fortify Parham and Munford. The Southern troops were as well positioned as possible and began to lob artillery on the Federal troops organizing in Burkittsville.

After a bit of brief reconnaissance, General Franklin opted for Crampton's Gap as the point of attack. Colonel Bartlett's division was ordered to lead the assault. He ordered his troops forward at 4:00 in the afternoon. He had two brigades totaling 1,400 men and organized them into two battle lines. The front line consisted of just the 27th New York infantry, who he sent ahead as skirmishers. Following behind were the 16th New York and the 5th Maine regiments. Behind Bartlett's brigade was that of Newton, with Torbert's New Jersey brigade following last.

In all there were six lines of troops advancing on the Confederate line, in addition to the men of the 96th Pennsylvania, who were still engaged with Munford's Virginia skirmishers. A member

---

[51] *OR*, series I, vol. 19, part I, 826.
[52] *OR*, series I, vol. 19, part I, 873.

of the 96[53], Captain John Boyle, forged ahead with his regiment against a sound defensive Confederate force. Although the Federals greatly outnumbered the Confederates, Boyle noted that "the rebel position was probably one of the strongest and, naturally, most defensive positions held by either party during the war, and one of the most difficult to surmount."[53] Not only did the Union men have to contend with inhospitable terrain, they were additionally tasked with surviving amidst sniper fire and artillery from above.

The 27th New York regiment advanced to skirmish and was quickly attacked by the hidden sharpshooters, artillery and fire from the battle line of Parham and Munford. They were engaged in a tremendously fierce fight while the 96th Pennsylvania, after more than three hours of fighting, began to fall back. The 27th soon found themselves in a similar battle, and due to the severity of the fighting, they began to exhaust their stores of ammunition. They too were ordered to fall back and along with the men of the 96th Pennsylvania, they sought protection behind any object available. Colonel Bartlett ordered the 16th New York and 5th Maine forward to replace the two regiments that had just withdrawn. The firing of rifles and muskets was without pause, remembered George Bicknell of the 5th Maine, "Almost every moment, some poor fellow in our lines was struck down by the fire of the rebs."[54]

Newton's brigade soon moved forward in support of Bartlett's men and courageously, the 96th Pennsylvania returned to the line with little respite. Once the 96th rejoined the line, the entirety of Slocum's division was engaged with the Confederate troops. Incredibly, the Rebel soldiers were able to maintain their position and occupy their Federal counterparts. Frustration grew among the Union commanders, which prompted General Slocum to order the 1st Maryland Light Artillery Forward in order to puncture the Confederate line. Immediately upon arrival, the artillerists were pelted by rebel fire and forced to abandon their guns. With this news, General Franklin began to fear that Slocum's left flank was on the verge of being turned and thusly ordered Smith's 2nd Division to "throw a brigade to the left of the pass."[55] With this order, Smith deployed Brigadier General William Brooks' brigade ahead. The Confederate forces still rained fire down on the advancing Yankees and their line held. Finally, at 5:20 that afternoon, Colonels Bartlett and Torbert, whose men were nearly deplete of ammunition, order a full bayonet charge at the quick. Torbert's New Jersey troops led the charge and at last, the Confederates were forced to retreat.

When the men of the 96th Pennsylvania alit on the final field they were tasked to cross, the concealed men of Holt's 10th Georgia fired in unison at the Pennsylvanians from a mere 20 paces away. Cake was incensed and proceeded to order his own bayonet charge. The 96th at last breached the wall that acted as a barrier for the Georgians and the combatants were briefly

---

[53] John T. Boyle, "The Ninety-sixth at Crampton's Pass, September 14, 1862," *Philadelphia Weekly Times,* September 30, 1871.

[54] George W. Bicknell, *History of the Fifth Maine Volunteers* (Portland, ME: H.L. Davis, 1871), 139.

[55] *OR,* series I, vol. 19, part I, 401.

engaged in close quarter combat that included fists, gun butts, and knives.[56] Meanwhile, Brooks and his Vermont men charged Munford's line south of the Burkittsville Pike and quickly eliminated the Confederate line.

As the rebel soldiers were fleeing up the slope, General Cobb's men were forming to their rear. By five o'clock, the general had deployed the 15th North Carolina regiment in addition to the 16th and 24th Georgia infantry men and his namesake regiment, Cobb's Legion, commanded by Lieutenant Colonel Jefferson Lamar, in a battle line parallel to and behind what was previously Parham's line.[57]

Cobb's line did not hold for very long. Fast approaching on the Confederate left was the indomitable 96th Pennsylvania, followed from behind and to the left by the 32nd, 18th, and 16th New York regiments. Cobb's line was immediately thrust into confusion as the retreating soldiers of Parham's line comingled with Cobb's men, who in turn followed in retreat. The troops that remained were no match for the Federal attackers and the Confederate line soon crumbled and scattered.

Fittingly, Cake's 96th Pennsylvania men were the first to reach the summit at Crampton's Gap. The frantic Confederates mounted a futile artillery attempt that lasted but minutes as they were swiftly forced to withdraw, leaving one of their guns behind. By 6:45 that evening, the Union troops were in complete control of the gap and Cobb's men were in a full and fast retreat down the western slope of the mountain into Pleasant Valley.

Although this gap battle was brief in relation to the struggle that transpired at Fox's and Turner's Gaps, the casualties were high. The total number of Confederate troops engaged at Crampton's Gap was 2,450. The recorded casualties numbered approximately 1,000 men, 600 of who were captured and taken prisoner. The Union also suffered a great number considering they overwhelming force with which they attacked. Two men were listed as missing and 418 were wounded while 113 were killed in action.

In General Slocum's official report, he boasted, "Although greatly reduced in numbers by losses on the Peninsula, although fatigued by long marches and constant service…each regiment indeed, every man   did his whole duty, not reluctantly, but with that eagerness and enthusiasm which rendered success certain."[58]

Lee was less enthusiastic and sent a much more succinct message to General McLaws that evening. Not knowing the fate of Jackson at Harpers Ferry, he simply informed his general, "The day has gone against us and this army will go by Sharpsburg and cross the river there."[59]

---

[56] Hoptak, 151.

[57] John H. Eicher and David J. Eicher, *Civil War High Commands* (Stanford, CA: Stanford University Press, 2001), 178.

[58] *OR*, series I, vol. 19, part I, 381.

Lee later reported about the fighting at South Mountain: "The effort to force the passage of the mountains had failed, but it was manifest that without re-enforcements we could not hazard a renewal of the engagement, as the enemy could easily turn either flank. Information was also received that another large body of Federal troops had during the afternoon forced their way through Crampton's Gap, only 5 miles in rear of McLaws. Under these circumstances, it was determined to retire to Sharpsburg, where we would be upon the flank and rear of the enemy should he move against McLaws, and where we could more readily unite with the rest of the army. This movement was efficiently and skillfully covered by the cavalry brigade of General Fitzhugh Lee, and was accomplished without interruption by the enemy, who did not appear on the west side of the pass at Boonsborough until about 8 a.m. on the following morning. The resistance that had been offered to the enemy at Boonsborough secured sufficient time to enable General Jackson to complete the reduction of Harper's Ferry."

After the Confederate troops retreated from Crampton's Gap, General McLaws attempted to construct an ad hoc battle line in Pleasant Valley in order to detain the Federal troops in their presumed advanced into Harpers Ferry. Lee declined McLaws suggestion, as he had not yet heard from General Jackson and was unaware that the Federal garrison was on the verge of surrender. Thus, Lee believed that the best course of action to protect his army in order to fight another day, was to retreat back into Virginia. He instructed all his commanders to order their troops off the mountain. The plan was to regather in Sharpsburg and retreat en masse into Virginia. General McClellan; however, was also unaware of hire dire the situation had become for Miles at Harpers Ferry and boasted that he had forced Lee on a panicked retreat back to southern soil. As McClellan wired President Lincoln in celebration, lauding himself as the hero, Lee somberly ordered his men to withdraw.

At 10:00 the night of September 14, the first Confederate troops made their way down the slope of South Mountain. Colquitt's men were the first to leave, followed in order by Rodes, Garland, Ripley, and G.B. Anderson. Before 1:00 a.m. on the 15th, Drayton, Hood, Tige Anderson, Kemper, Garnett, and Evans had all withdrawn their men. Jenkins' troops were the last to leave at 4:00 a.m.

Lee's plans for a triumphant northern invasion withered as the sun rose, but just at that hour, a courier General Jackson had dispatched the previous evening reached Lee in Sharpsburg with the news that Harpers Ferry was on the brink of surrender and that Jackson's troops would be free to support Lee and Longstreet. Upon hearing this news, Lee altered his plans to retreat and informed his generals, "We will make our stand on these hills."[60]

Ambrose Burnside, who would play a controversial role at Antietam, believed that South

---

[59] OR, series I, vol. 51, part II, 618.
[60] Joseph L. Harsh, Taken at the Flood: Robert E. Lee and Confederate Strategy in the Maryland Campaign of 1862 (Kent, OH: Kent State University Press, 1999), 305.

Mountain had been a "brilliant" success, writing in his post-campaign report:

"Early on the morning of the 14th, General Pleasonton commenced his reconnaissance of Turner's Gap and South Mountain, assisted by Cox's division, supported by Willcox's division, of General Reno's corps, and found the enemy in force. General Pleasonton had reconnoitered the ground fully, and, after posting Benjamin's and Gibson's batteries on the high grounds immediately in front of the gap, indicated to Cox's division the road that should be taken in order to turn the enemy's right. This division and Willcox's division became engaged immediately.

Soon after, I arrived on the ground with General Reno, and directed him to order up General Rodman's and General Sturgis' division to sup port Cox's division, which had passed up to the left of the main gap by the Sharpsburg road over the South Mountain. After these divisions had passed on to the front, General Reno moved on and took the immediate command of his corps. Soon after, General Hooker's corps arrived, composed of the divisions of Generals Meade, Ricketts, Hatch, and Doubleday, and I ordered it to move up to the right of the main pike, by the Old Hagerstown road, and, if possible, turn the enemy's left and get in his rear. At the same time I detached from his corps General Gibbon's brigade, with Captain Campbell's battery, for the purpose of making a demonstration upon the enemy's center, up the main pike, as soon as the movements of Generals Hooker and Reno had sufficiently progressed. At the same time 1 sent orders to General Reno, whose corps had been sharply engaged all the morning, to move upon the enemy's position with his whole three as soon as I informed him that General Hooker was well advanced up the crest of the mountain on our right.

About this time the general commanding arrived on the ground, and I repeated to him my dispositions, which he fully approved. He remained at my headquarters during the remainder of the engagement, and I reported to him, personally, all the orders that I gave from that time.

The orders given to both Generals Hooker and Reno were most skillfully and successfully executed, after which General Gibbon was ordered forward just before sunset, and succeeded in pushing his command up the main road to within a short distance of the crest of the main pass, during which movement he had a most brilliant engagement after night-fall, our forces gradually driving the enemy before them.

At this time, say 8 p.m., the enemy had been driven from their strong positions, and the firing ceased, except upon our extreme left, where General Reno's division, then under command of General Cox (General Reno having been killed about 7 p.m.), were partially engaged till 10 o'clock.

My command, having been engaged for a greater part of the day upon the crests of the mountain without water, and many without food, were very much exhausted. Nevertheless they maintained their positions, and were ready on the following morning for an advance on the enemy, who had retreated in the direction of Sharpsburg during the night."

Hooker

South Mountain was the first major pitched battle between the two sides in September, and the Union had given as good as it got, prompting *The New York World* to write that the battle at South Mountain would "turn back the tide of rebel successes" and report that "the strength of the rebels is hopelessly broken."

Chapter 7: The Aftermath of South Mountain

Lee braced himself for renewed hostilities on September 15, but McClellan remained cautious and did not attack the Confederates that day, allowing Jackson to finish off the garrison at Harpers Ferry and make his way back to Lee on September 16. By that point, Lee had already decided to pull back his army to Sharpsburg, with its back to the Potomac River and its front along Antietam Creek, affording his army at least one natural obstacle separating his army from McClellan's.

McClellan's lead elements arrived around Sharpsburg on the night of September 15, and the rest of the army came up on September 16, but McClellan did not order a general attack that day out of fear that he was still heavily outnumbered. Had he done so, he would not only have had an overwhelming advantage but would not have had to deal with A.P. Hill's Light Division, which was still busy at Harpers Ferry. Lee wrote of McClellan's movements on the 16th: "On the 16th the artillery fire became warmer, and continued throughout the day. The enemy crossed the Antietam beyond the reach of our batteries and menaced our left. In anticipation of this movement, Hood's two brigades had been transferred from the right and posted between D. H. Hill and the Hagerstown road. General Jackson was now directed to take position on Hood's left, and formed his line with his right resting upon the Hagerstown road and his left extending toward the Potomac, protected by General Stuart with the cavalry and horse artillery. General Walker, with his two brigades, was stationed on Longstreet's right. As evening approached, the enemy opened more vigorously with his artillery, and bore down heavily with his infantry upon Hood, but the attack was gallantly repulsed. At 10 p.m. Hood's troops were relieved by the brigades of Lawton and Trimble, of Ewell's division, commanded by General Lawton. Jackson's own division, under General J. R. Jones, was on Lawton's left, supported by the remaining brigades of Ewell."

With McClellan's men all in position on the night of the 16th, McClellan decided to give general battle on the 17th. Longstreet described the scene before the battle commenced: "The blue uniforms of the federals appeared among the trees that crowned the heights on the eastern bank of the Antietam. The number increased, and larger and larger grew the field of blue until is seemed to stretch as far as the eye could see, and from the tops of the mountains down to the edge of the stream gathered the great army of McClellan."

Still operating under the belief that he was outnumbered, McClellan's plan was to break Lee's left flank in the northern sector, because the crosses that he knew about over Antietam Creek (Burnside's Bridge and the bridge leading to Boonsboro) were held on the other side by Confederates who could operate along the high ground. McClellan's cavalry had not scouted other passes along Antietam Creek, and he and his officers seemed to be unaware that the Antietam Creek was so shallow in places around those bridges that the men could have waded across without trying to squeeze across bridges.

Worried about being outnumbered, McClellan's plan called for an assault with only half his army, starting with two corps along the Confederate left, and the support of perhaps a third or fourth corps. Meanwhile, he initially planned to launch diversionary attacks in the center and the Confederate right. However, the late night skirmishing and probing conducted by men of Hooker's I Corps on the night of the 16th suggested to Lee that they would attack there in force on the morning of the 17th, and before the battle he bolstered his left flank. He also sent word to A.P. Hill and Lafayette McLaws to force march with all haste to Sharpsburg.

As Lee had guessed, and as McClellan intended, the Battle of Antietam began near dawn on the morning of the 17th, with the advance of Hooker's I Corps down the Hagerstown Turnpike toward the small white Dunker Church, a small one room building that served as a church for a small group of German Baptists. Initially opposing Hooker's 8,500 man Corps were Stonewall Jackson's men, which numbered just under 8,000. Jackson's defenders were deployed across the Turnpike in the West Woods on the left, and a cornfield on the right.

The Dunker Church in the background

Hooker decided to start the fighting with an artillery bombardment due to the fact that the nature of the terrain made it unclear what his corps would be facing in the cornfield and the West Woods. Hooker's men could see the Confederates' bayonets shining in the cornfield, but the corn was high enough to conceal their number. During the artillery duel, infantry pushed forward until there was a fierce pitched battle in the cornfield, including hand-to-hand fighting. Colonel Benjamin Cook of the 12th Massachusetts later recalled his experience in the cornfield as "the most deadly fire of the war. Rifles are shot to pieces in the hands of the soldiers, canteens and haversacks are riddled with bullets, the dead and wounded go down in scores."

Despite Jackson's valiant defense, the Union advance kept pushing forward along the West Woods and the Turnpike, and Jackson's line was on the verge of collapse by 7:00 a.m. In one of the most legendary parts of the battle, John Bell Hood's Texans had come up to the field and had not eaten breakfast, so they were held in reserve and allowed to start preparing a meal. Just before they could eat, however, they were called into action, infuriating his men. Thankfully for the Confederates, it would be the Union who felt the brunt of their fury.

Hood

Hood's division helped the Confederates stave off the first major assault in the West Woods, and Hooker's attack fizzled out in part because Hooker was seriously injured during the fighting. Hooker had been seemingly everywhere during the fighting, and many of his comrades believed that Antietam would have turned out differently had he not been injured. Before his injury, Hooker said of the cornfield, "every stalk of corn in the northern and greater part of the field was cut as closely as could have been done with a knife, and the slain lay in rows precisely as they had stood in their ranks a few moments before." Hooker was replaced by George Meade, who would ironically also replace Hooker as commander of the Army of the Potomac before Gettysburg.

Hooker's I Corps was relieved by the XII Corps under Joseph Mansfield, who had been promoted to Corps command just a few days earlier and was so new to command and unfamiliar with the terrain that he advanced his men in a file that was 10 ranks deep instead of the normal 2-rank-deep battle line. On top of that, Mansfield got confused by Confederate fire from the cornfield, mistakenly believing that it was friendly fire. And once he got all the necessary information and the delays sorted out, he was mortally wounded.

Mansfield

As the XII Corps struggled, Edwin Sumner's II Corps began an unsupported and uncoordinated attack from the east, entering the East Woods in confusion. Like Mansfield, Sumner's battle line was comprised unusually and made an inviting target for Confederate artillery. The Corps suffered over 2,000 casualties in half an hour, with division commander John Sedgwick suffering a serious injury. Sumner has long been criticized for the lack of coordination and the unusual battle formation.

By 10:00 a.m., over 13,000 men had become casualties in just 4 hours, and two Union corps commanders were out of the fight.

As if the fighting in the north wasn't fierce enough, the fighting at midday would turn one sunken road into "Bloody Lane". Having been repulsed in the north, the next Union attacks focused on the center of the Confederate line, beginning ironically with a division of Sumner's II Corps which had gotten lost in the East Woods during the attack in the north and ventured south. With Sumner's II Corps advancing in a disorderly fashion and being badly repulsed, Sumner initially asked French's lost division to make a diversionary attack on the center.

There French's men found D.H. Hill's division, which after South Mountain was reduced to only about 2,500 men itself. On top of that, some of Hill's brigades had reinforced Jackson's men during the morning, meaning French had veered right into the most lightly defended part of the Confederate line. However, Hill's men were protected by the features of the "sunken road", a dirt road that had been worn down over the years by wagons and thus formed a sort of trench that made defensive warfare much safer.

The dead in the Bloody Lane

As the fighting in the center raged, Col. Francis C. Barlow and 350 men from two New York regiments took a commanding position that oversaw the sunken road and allowed them to pour in a deadly flanking fire that enfiladed the Confederate line. Miscommunication by the Confederates over how to face this threat inadvertently resulted in an entire brigade marching toward the rear back toward Sharpsburg, breaking the Confederate line.

At this point, it was about 1:00 p.m., and in the middle another 5,500 casualties had been incurred. As the broken Confederate line started retreating, Franklin's VI Corps, comprised of 12,000 men, were ready to advance on the center. In the field, Franklin's request to advance was denied by Edwin Sumner, who in addition to commanding the II Corps was in command of the "grand division", making him responsible for that wing of the army thanks to the unwieldy structure of the Army of the Potomac's leadership. Franklin thus had to attempt to make the request to McClellan himself, whose headquarters were over a mile to the rear, costing precious time. McClellan personally rode to the area, listened to both men's arguments, and decided to hold Franklin's men in place, still clearly concerned that he was outnumbered.

Lee's army may ultimately have been saved by the Northern army's inability to cross the creek near "Burnside's Bridge". Ambrose Burnside had been given command of the "Right Wing" of the Army of the Potomac (the I Corps and IX Corps) at the start of the Maryland Campaign for the Battle of South Mountain, but McClellan separated the two corps at the Battle of Antietam, placing them on opposite ends of the Union battle line. However, Burnside continued to act as though he was a wing commander instead of a corps commander, so instead of directly commanding his IX corps, he funneled orders through General Jacob D. Cox. This poor organization contributed to the corps's hours-long delay in attacking and crossing what is now called "Burnside's Bridge" on the right flank of the Confederate line.

Making matters worse, Burnside did not perform adequate reconnaissance of the area, which afforded several easy fording sites of the creek out of range of the Army of Northern Virginia. Instead of unopposed crossings, his troops were forced into repeated assaults across the narrow bridge which was dominated by Confederate sharpshooters on high ground across the bridge. On top of that, Burnside's failure to have his men wade across meant that they were easily repulsed a couple of times trying to force their way across the bridge. McClellan got so fed up that he began sending couriers, and at one point he ordered an aide, "Tell him if it costs 10,000 men he must go now." Burnside reacted angrily, "McClellan appears to think I am not trying my best to carry this bridge; you are the third or fourth one who has been to me this morning with similar orders." As Confederate staff officer Henry Kyd Douglas later pointed out, "Go and look at [Burnside's Bridge], and tell me if you don't think Burnside and his corps might have executed a hop, skip, and jump and landed on the other side. One thing is certain, they might have waded it that day without getting their waist belts wet in any place."

Eventually, after about three hours and several attempts, the Union men pushed their way across, but once they were on the other side of the Antietam they delayed yet again to regroup. After two hours attempting to get ammunition across the bridge, Burnside's men began another general advance against the Confederate right, which by now had been reinforced by every conceivable unit Lee could muster. Meanwhile, A.P. Hill's men were on the march and nearing the vicinity. They had intended to be brought up to the Confederate left, but Lee ordered him to come up on the Confederate right instead.

As Hill's men neared Boteler's Ford, the best available route across the Potomac for the Confederates, Burnside began shifting his men around the Confederate right even though he heavily outnumbered them, in the hopes that a move on Boteler's Ford would cut Lee's army off and trap it along the Potomac. Around 3:00 p.m., Burnside ordered nearly 8,000 fresh soldiers to push west, and meanwhile the streets of Sharpsburg were filled with retreating Confederates. Lee's army was disorganized and on the verge of being broken.

As Burnside's men pushed in on his right flank, Lee turned to see dust from a unit marching from the southwest. Had they been Union men, his entire army may have been bagged at

Sharpsburg, and when Lee asked whose troops they were, one of his aides assured him, "They are flying the Virginia flags." Lee excitedly announced, "It is A.P. Hill from Harpers Ferry!"

With Hill crashing down on his left flank, Burnside lost his nerve, even though the IX Corps still heavily outnumbered Hill's Light Division even after incurring 20% casualties during the day already. Burnside ordered a general retreat back to Antietam Creek and waited there while requesting more reinforcements from McClellan, who informed him, "I can do nothing more. I have no infantry." When told he had repulsed men under the command of Burnside, his West Point friend, Hill was reportedly asked if he knew his old classmate, to which he responded, "Ought to! He owes me eight thousand dollars!" Hill had allegedly loaned the money to Burnside in their friendlier antebellum days.

Of course, McClellan's assertion that he had no infantry was not entirely true. By the end of the afternoon, Union attacks on the flanks and the center of the line had been violent but eventually unsuccessful. Aware that his army was badly bloodied but fearing Lee had many more men than he did, McClellan refused to commit fresh reserves from Franklin's VI Corps or Fitz-John Porter's V Corps. McClellan's decision was probably sealed by Fitz John Porter telling him, "Remember, General, I command the last reserve of the last Army of the Republic." Thus, the day ended in a tactical stalemate, with the Union suffering nearly 12,500 casualties (including over 2,000 dead) and the Confederates suffering over 10,000 casualties (including over 1,500 dead). Nearly 1/4th of the Army of the Potomac had been injured, captured or killed, and the same could be said for nearly 1/3rd of Lee's Army of Northern Virginia. It was the deadliest and bloodiest day in American history.

After the battle, McClellan wrote to his wife, "Those in whose judgment I rely tell me that I fought the battle splendidly and that it was a masterpiece of art. ... I feel I have done all that can be asked in twice saving the country. ... I feel some little pride in having, with a beaten & demoralized army, defeated Lee so utterly. ... Well, one of these days history will I trust do me justice." Historians have generally been far less kind with their praise, criticizing McClellan for not sharing his battle plans with his corps commanders, which prevented them from using initiative outside of their sectors. McClellan also failed to use cavalry in the battle; had cavalry been used for reconnaissance, other fording options might have prevented the debacle at Burnside's Bridge. As historian Stephen Sears would point out in his seminal book about the Maryland Campaign, "In making his battle against great odds to save the Republic, General McClellan had committed barely 50,000 infantry and artillerymen to the contest. A third of his army did not fire a shot. Even at that, his men repeatedly drove the Army of Northern Virginia to the brink of disaster, feats of valor entirely lost on a commander thinking of little beyond staving off his own defeat."

On the morning of September 18, Lee's army prepared to defend against a Union assault that ultimately never came. Finally, an improvised truce was declared to allow both sides to

MC seeks my II.

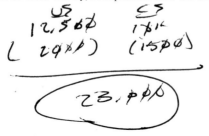
US
12,500
(2000)

CS
1800
(1500)

23,000

exchange their wounded. That evening, Lee's forces began withdrawing across the Potomac to return to Virginia.

McClellan made one push against Lee's army at nearby Shepherdstown. Shortly before dusk on September 19, Union Brig. General Charles Griffin sent 2,000 infantry and sharpshooters from Maj. General Fitz-John Porter's V Corps across the Potomac River at Boteler's Ford (also known as Shepardstown Ford) in pursuit, only to pull them back the following day when Stonewall Jackson's men entered the fray. However, Union General Adelbert Ames had mistakenly received orders to advance across the Potomac into Virginia, so he sent the 20th Maine regiment wading into the water, which actually encountered retreating Union troops as they did, and they were promptly fired upon by a barrage of Confederate artillery.

The 20th Maine would become famous at Gettysburg, but here they had no fighting chance. Just as soon as Joshua Lawrence Chamberlain's 20th had crossed, their bugles sounded retreat. Remaining calm atop his horse, Chamberlain redirected his men back across the river, "steadying his men through a deep place in the river where several of the Fifth New York were drowned in his presence." And although Lieutenant Colonel Chamberlain had his horse shot out from under him, he succeeded in returning his regiment safely back to shore with only three casualties suffering minor wounds, his ability to remain calm under pressure now apparent.

As the Battle of Shepherdstown indicated, Lee's rear guard was formidable enough that officers throughout the Army of the Potomac concurred with McClellan's actions not to go after the Army of Northern Virginia. Lee's army then moved toward the Shenandoah Valley while the Army of the Potomac hovered around Sharpsburg.

Although Antietam ended as a tactical draw, the Maryland Campaign is now widely considered a turning point in the Civil War. It resulted in forcing Lee's army out of Maryland and back into Virginia, making it a strategic victory for the North and an opportune time for President Abraham Lincoln to issue the Emancipation Proclamation. James McPherson would summarize the critical importance of the Maryland Campaign: "No other campaign and battle in the war had such momentous, multiple consequences as Antietam. In July 1863 the dual Union triumphs at Gettysburg and Vicksburg struck another blow that blunted a renewed Confederate offensive in the East and cut off the western third of the Confederacy from the rest. In September 1864 Sherman's capture of Atlanta reversed another decline in Northern morale and set the stage for the final drive to Union victory. These also were pivotal moments. But they would never have happened if the triple Confederate offensives in Mississippi, Kentucky, and most of all Maryland had not been defeated in the fall of 1862."

Although McClellan is often criticized for the way he conducted the fighting at Antietam, Lee has not gone without criticism either. Longstreet's artillery chief, Porter Alexander, who would be tasked with conducting the artillery bombardment before Pickett's Charge at Gettysburg, was extremely critical of Lee for the Maryland Campaign, writing in his memoirs:

"Lee's hopes were by no means so exaggerated as McClellan's fears. He counted upon no hope from Maryland, until his own army should have demonstrated its ability to maintain itself within the state. He hardly hoped for more than 'to detain the enemy upon the northern frontier until the approach of winter should render his advance into Virginia difficult, if not impracticable.' But he did entertain hopes of a decisive victory here on a field more remote from a safe place of refuge for the enemy than his victories of the Seven Days and of 2d Manassas had been. The hope would have been reasonable had his army been larger and his armament better, but under all the circumstances and conditions it was as improbable of realization as the chance of an earthquake would have been. He did, indeed, win a complete victory over all the infantry which the enemy engaged, but their position was more favorable to prevent his making a counter-stroke than was his to resist their attack. Their heavy guns across the Antietam gave him protection, just as at Fredericksburg the Federal artillery on the Stafford heights, afterward in two battles, safely covered the Federal infantry on the opposite shore.

Briefly, Lee took a great risk for no chance of gain except the killing of some thousands of his enemy with the loss of, perhaps, two-thirds as many of his own men. That was a losing game for the Confederacy. Its supply of men was limited; that of the enemy was not. That was not war! Yet now, who would have it otherwise? History must be history and could not afford to lose this battle from its records. For the nation is immortal and will forever prize and cherish the record made that day by both sides, as actors in the boldest and the bloodiest battle ever fought upon this continent."

Lincoln and McClellan meeting after Antietam

McClellan had successfully removed Lee's army from Maryland, but he had failed to knock Lee's army out while it was on the ropes. When Lee escaped back to Virginia without pursuit, the Lincoln Administration was greatly frustrated.

Despite heavily outnumbering the Southern army and badly damaging it at Antietam, McClellan never did pursue Lee across the Potomac, citing shortages of equipment and the fear of overextending his forces. General-in-Chief Henry W. Halleck wrote in his official report, "The long inactivity of so large an army in the face of a defeated foe, and during the most favorable season for rapid movements and a vigorous campaign, was a matter of great disappointment and regret." Lincoln sardonically referred to the Army of the Potomac as General McClellan's bodyguard, and in one October message to McClellan, Lincoln didn't bother trying to conceal his disgust, writing, "I have just read your dispatch about sore-tongued and fatigued horses, Will you pardon me for asking what the horses of your army have done since the Battle of Antietam that fatigues anything?"

Some of Lincoln's assertions make clear his lack of familiarity with military matters. McClellan still had to deal with the logistical reorganization of his army and the rehabilitation after having suffered about 10,000 casualties in one day. And as Lincoln grew more disenchanted with McClellan, specifically the state of inertia along the Potomac, JEB Stuart rode around McClellan's army for the second time in early October, displaying just how unable the Union forces were to cover the Potomac crossings.

McClellan also faced growing public pressure and pressure from the Administration to advance before the midterm elections. McClellan wished to wait until Spring of 1863 to resume active campaigning, hoping once again to use the Peninsula, but he was compelled to move by mid-October. McClellan saw the campaign as merely a temporary way of placating the Administration before positioning his army around Fredericksburg to plan for the following Spring.

Lincoln had finally had enough of McClellan's "slows", and his constant excuses for not taking forward action. Lincoln relieved McClellan of his command of the Army of the Potomac on November 7, 1862, effectively ending the general's military career. Once again using the media to deflect his inadequacies, McClellan blamed Washington for having not sent more men and equipment before mounting the Antietam offensive. Lincoln reportedly responded, "Sending reinforcements to McClellan is like shoveling flies across a barn." McClellan's military career was essentially over, having ended in disgrace.

Ironically, when McClellan was removed, the army was at a highpoint in terms of morale, and McClellan was starting to understand that if the Administration wouldn't allow a transfer of his army onto the Peninsula, he would have to continue sliding east along the overland route using available railroads, which is similar in scope to Ulysses S. Grant's 1864 Overland Campaign. But it was not to be for another 2 years, and on November 7, 1862, McClellan was replaced by Ambrose Burnside, one of the subordinates most responsible for the shortcomings of the Maryland campaign.

Online Resources

Other books about the Civil War by Charles River Editors

Other books about South Mountain on Amazon

Other books about Antietam on Amazon

Bibliography

Bicknell, George W. *History of the Fifth Maine Volunteers.* Portland, ME: H.L. Davis, 1871.

Bosbyshell, Oliver Christian. *The 48th in the War.* Philadelphia: Avil Printing Company, 1895.

Boyle, John T. "The Ninety-sixth at Crampton's Pass, September 14, 1862." *Philadelphia*

Weekly Times, September 30, 1871.

Cox, Jacob Dolson. *Military Reminiscences of the Civil War.* 2 vols. New York: Scribner's,
1900.

Dawes, Rufus R. *Service with the Sixth Wisconsin Volunteers.* Marietta, OH: Alderman &
Sons,
1890.

Eicher, David J. *The Longest Night: A Military History of the Civil War.* New York: Simon &
Schuster, 2001.

Eicher, David J. and David J. Eicher. *Civil War High Commands.* Stanford, CA: Stanford
University Press, 2001.

Harsh, Joseph L. *Taken at the Flood: Robert E. Lee and Confederate Strategy in the Maryland
Campaign of 1862.* Kent, OH: Kent State University Press, 1999.

Hayes, Rutherford B. *Diary and Letters of Rutherford B. Hayes: Nineteenth President of the
United States.* Vol. 2, 1861-1865. Edited by Charles Richard Williams. New York:
Kraus Reprint Company, 1971.

Hill, Daniel Harvey. "The Battle of South Mountain, or Boonsboro." In *Battles and Leaders
Of the Civil War.* 3 vols. New York: The Century Company, 1887-1888.

Hoptak, John David. *The Battle of South Mountain.* Charleston, SC: The History Press, 2011.

Lane, David. *A Soldiers Diary: The Story of a Volunteer, 1862-1865.* Jackson, MI, 1905.

Longstreet, James. *From Manassas to Appomattox: Memoirs of the Civil War in America.*
Philadelphia: J.B. Lippincott Co., 1896.

McClellan, George B. *The Civil War Papers of George B. McClellan: Selected
Correspondence,*
1860-1865. Edited by Stephen W. Sears. New York: Ticknor & Fields, 1989.

McPherson, James. *Antietam: The Battle That Changed the Course of the Civil War.*

New York: Oxford University Press, 2002.

Rafuse, Ethan. *Antietam, South Mountain, & Harpers Ferry: A Battlefield Guide.* Lincoln:

University of Nebraska Press, 2008.

Slotkin, Richard. *The Long Road to Antietam: How the Civil War Became a Revolution.*

New York: W.W. Norton & Company, 2012.

Syphert, J.R. *History of the Pennsylvania Reserve Corps.* Lancaster, PA: Elias Barr, 1865.

United States War Department. *The War of the Rebellion: A Compilation of the Official Records*

Of the Union and Confederate Armies, 128 vols. Washington, D.C.: Government

Printing Office, 1888.

Free Books by Charles River Editors

We have brand new titles available for free most days of the week. To see which of our titles are currently free, click on this link.

Discounted Books by Charles River Editors

We have titles at a discount price of just 99 cents everyday. To see which of our titles are currently 99 cents, click on this link.

Made in the USA
Middletown, DE
30 December 2020

30462893R00040